麦格希 **中英双语阅读文库**

破解世纪悬疑

【美】比林斯 (Billings, H.)　　【美】比林斯 (Billings, M.) ●主编

杨挺扬 ●译

麦格希中英双语阅读文库编委会 ●编

全国百佳图书出版单位
吉林出版集团股份有限公司

图书在版编目（CIP）数据

破解世纪悬疑 / (美) 比林斯 (Billings. H),
(美) 比林斯 (Billings. M) 主编；麦格希中英双
语阅读文库编委会编；杨挺扬译. -- 2版. -- 长春：
吉林出版集团股份有限公司, 2018.3（2022.1重印）
（麦格希中英双语阅读文库）
ISBN 978-7-5581-4730-2

Ⅰ.①破… Ⅱ.①比… ②比… ③麦… ④杨… Ⅲ.
①英语—汉语—对照读物②科学知识—青少年读物 Ⅳ.
①H319.4：Z

中国版本图书馆CIP数据核字(2018)第046128号

破解世纪悬疑

编	麦格希中英双语阅读文库编委会
插 画	齐 航　李延霞
责任编辑	沈丽娟
封面设计	冯冯翼
开 本	660mm × 960mm　1/16
字 数	237千字
印 张	10.5
版 次	2018年3月第2版
印 次	2022年1月第2次印刷

出 版	吉林出版集团股份有限公司
发 行	吉林出版集团外语教育有限公司
地 址	长春市福祉大路5788号龙腾国际大厦B座7层
电 话	总编办：0431-81629929
	发行部：0431-81629927　0431-81629921(Fax)
印 刷	北京一鑫印务有限责任公司

ISBN 978-7-5581-4730-2　定价：38.00元

前言 PREFACE

　　英国思想家培根说过：阅读使人深刻。阅读的真正目的是获取信息，开拓视野和陶冶情操。从语言学习的角度来说，学习语言若没有大量阅读就如隔靴搔痒，因为阅读中的语言是最丰富、最灵活、最具表现力、最符合生活情景的，同时读物中的情节、故事引人入胜，进而能充分调动读者的阅读兴趣，培养读者的文学修养，至此，语言的学习水到渠成。

　　"麦格希中英双语阅读文库"在世界范围内选材，涉及科普、社会文化、文学名著、传奇故事、成长励志等多个系列，充分满足英语学习者课外阅读之所需，在阅读中学习英语、提高能力。

　　◎难度适中

　　本套图书充分照顾读者的英语学习阶段和水平，从读者的阅读兴趣出发，以难易适中的英语语言为立足点，选材精心、编排合理。

◎精品荟萃

本套图书注重经典阅读与实用阅读并举。既包含国内外脍炙人口、耳熟能详的美文，又包含科普、人文、故事、励志类等多学科的精彩文章。

◎功能实用

本套图书充分体现了双语阅读的功能和优势，充分考虑到读者课外阅读的方便，超出核心词表的词汇均出现在使其意义明显的语境之中，并标注释义。

鉴于编者水平有限，凡不周之处，谬误之处，皆欢迎批评教正。

我们真心地希望本套图书承载的文化知识和英语阅读的策略对提高读者的英语著作欣赏水平和英语运用能力有所裨益。

丛书编委会

Contents

1

Death in the Tunnel

Falling Rocks!

Anyone who has driven through a mountain *region* has read a road sign like this one. Most people don't even notice such signs. If they do, they don't give them much thought. After all, what are the *odds* of being killed by a rock as it falls down a mountain?

Japanese media gather in front of the entrance to the Toyohama Tunnel shortly after the boulder fell.

飞来横祸
　　——隧道里的天灾

　　日本记者在砾石跌落不久聚集到了丰滨隧道入口前。

　　"小心落石！"

　　在山区驾驶过车的人都一定看到过这样的路标，但大多数都熟视无睹。即使他们看到了，也不会太在意。被山上滚落下来的石头砸死也未免太"幸运"了吧？

---

region　*n.* 地区

odds　*n.* 可能性；概率

If you think those odds are long, what would you say are the chances of being killed by a falling rock while driving through a *tunnel*? Believe it or not, it has happened. On February 10, 1996, a huge rock broke free from a mountain on the Japanese island of Hokkaido. It fell right onto the Toyohama Tunnel.

The rock that fell wasn't just a rock. It was a *boulder*. It weighed close to 50,000 tons. It was 210 feet tall and 120 feet wide. That made it as big as a 20-story building.

The falling boulder hit the top of the Toyohama Tunnel and crashed right through. At that exact moment, a car was passing through the tunnel. So was a bus carrying 19 people. About half of the people on the bus were *teenagers*. They came from the nearby fishing village of Furubira. They were on their way to a winter *carnival*. Both the bus and the car were pinned underneath the huge

---

如果你觉得这种可能性还是存在的话，那么驱车穿过隧道时被落石所伤的概率又有多大呢？信不信由你，这种事情的确发生过——1996年2月10日，位于日本北海道的一座山上，一块巨石跌落下来，正好砸在丰滨隧道上。

那不是一块普通的石头，而是重达5万吨、高210英尺、宽120英尺的砾岩磐石，它足有20层楼那么高大。

落下来的巨石掉到了丰滨隧道顶部并且直接砸穿隧道。恰在此时，一辆小汽车，还有一辆载有19人的公共汽车从隧道中经过。公共汽车里有一半是青少年，他们来自附近的古平町渔村，正打算去度冬季狂欢节。两辆车被死死地砸在了巨石的下面。

---

tunnel *n.* 隧道

teenager *n.* 青少年

boulder *n.* 巨石

carnival *n.* 狂欢节

boulder.

No one knows for sure why the boulder broke free. Perhaps a small earthquake had loosened it. There are many earthquakes in that part of Japan. Or perhaps the weather was to blame. It often snows in Hokkaido. When the snow *melts*, the water runs into cracks in the mountains. Then cold weather comes again, turning the water to ice. As the water becomes ice, it expands. It does so with enough force to crack a rock. Over many years, the ice could have opened a bigger and bigger *crack* in the mountain. In time, the ice could have loosened a boulder.

This was not the first massive boulder to fall in Hokkaido. Eighteen months earlier a boulder had fallen. It hit the ground not far from the Toyohama Tunnel. That boulder was twice as big as this one. Luckily, though, that one did not fall on anyone.

没有人能确定这块石头为什么会碎裂。可能是一次小规模的地震使它已经松动，日本的这个地带地震很频繁。或许应该归咎于天气——北海道经常下雪，雪融化成水以后就会流进山的裂缝里面。冷气再一次袭来的时候，裂缝里面的水又会结成冰。水结成冰，体积膨胀，这样它就有足够的力量使岩石碎裂。年复一年，冰在山上胀开了一条越来越大的裂缝，那时候冰就已经使这块巨石松动了。

巨大的山石已经不是第一次落到北海道了。18个月以前就掉过一块，那块石头有这块的两倍大，当时砸在距离丰滨隧道不远的地上，万幸的是它没有伤到任何人。

---

melt *v.* 融化   crack *n.* 裂缝

This time, 20 people were trapped under the boulder. Were any of them still alive? Rescuers managed to slip a tiny camera down through the *debris* into the tunnel. The camera showed parts of the crushed car and bus. It picked up no signs of life. But there was still the possibility that someone had survived. They had to get into the tunnel to find out. Everyone agreed it had to be done, but no one knew quite how to do it.

For 11 long hours, rescuers talked about what to do. At last, they decided not to dig straight through the tunnel. That would weaken the land above the tunnel's roof. Then they might have a second rockfall on their hands. Instead, they decided they would try to move the huge boulder. Then they could dig in through the top of the tunnel.

Meanwhile, friends and family members of the *victims* rushed to

---

这一次，20个人被困到了巨石之下，还能有生还者么？营救人员设法将一个小的摄像头穿过碎石滑入隧道之中，摄像机中显示了被压瘪的小汽车和公共汽车的一部分，却没有探测到生命存在的迹象。但是依然存在着有人还活着的可能性。他们必须进入到隧道里面去弄清楚，每个人都知道应该这样做，但是没人确切知道如何去做。

11个小时过去了，工作人员仍然在讨论如何开展营救。最后他们决定不直接挖通隧道，因为担心隧道顶上的土层变薄，会引起再一次的落石。相反，他们决定设法挪走那块巨石，这样他们可以从隧道顶上挖进去。

与此同时，遇难者的亲友们飞快地赶到了现场，在那里等候消息。不

---

debris *n.* 碎片；残骸　　　　　　　　　　victim *n.* 牺牲者；受害人

the site. There they waited for news. Soon it began to snow. The temperature fell quickly. "Hurry up! Please hurry up!" cried some of the people to the rescuers. They knew that if the rescuers didn't get into the tunnel soon, anyone still alive would freeze to death.

The rescuers decided to blast the boulder off the roof. With enough force, they could blow it into the sea below the tunnel. So they set off 550 pounds of *dynamite*. It was not enough. Only a tiny piece of the boulder broke off.

The rescuers could have used more dynamite. But they feared that too big a blast would cause a second rockfall. "We did not achieve our aim of removing the boulder because we cut the amount [of dynamite] for safety reasons," said one rescuer.

The next day, rescuers tried another *blast*. But again, only a small piece of the boulder broke off. The following day they tried a third

久，天开始下起雪来，气温迅速下降。"快点！求求你们了，快点吧！"亲友们带着哭腔向营救人员请求着。他们清楚如果不能及时进入隧道的话，即使里面的人没有被压死也会被冻死。

营救人员决定从顶上炸碎巨石。如果力量够大的话，就可以掀入到隧道下面的海里去，因此他们动用了550磅的炸药。但是这远远不够，只炸掉了一小片石头而已。

救援人员本可以加大药量的，但是他们担心爆炸太猛烈会导致再一次的岩体崩裂。"我们没有爆破成功的原因是出于考虑安全我们减少了炸药释放的剂量。"一名营救队员说。

第二天救援人员又进行了一次爆破，但又是只炸掉了一小块。接下来

dynamite *n.* 炸药   blast *n.* 爆炸

time. Still, they couldn't *topple* the rock. By this time, three days had passed. Family members and friends began to lose hope. "The past few days I've cried and cried while watching this unfold," said one relative. "I just don't have any more tears."

Some of the people became angry. They figured their loved ones inside the tunnel were dead by this time. All they wanted was to *retrieve* the bodies. "Even if they are dead, hurry up and pull them out of there," one person demanded.

On the fourth day, the rescuers blasted the boulder again. This time it worked. The explosion sent the boulder plunging down into the sea below the tunnel.

Even with the boulder gone, there was still a lot of work to do. The roof of the tunnel itself had to be cleared away. That took another two days. At last, on February 16, the rescuers reached the

---

的一天，他们进行了第三次尝试，可是依然没能奏效。此时，距离事故发生已经过去三天，家属和亲友们开始不抱希望了。"过去这几天我们在哭泣中守望着营救的进行，"一名亲属说，"现在眼泪已经哭干了。"

有一些人开始变得愤怒起来。他们觉得这个时候自己深爱的人在隧道里面已经死去了，而他们现在只是想得到尸体。"即使他们已经死了，快一点把他们从那里挖出来吧。"一个人命令道。

第四天的时候，营救人员又进行了一次爆破，这次奏效了，爆炸将巨大的砾石掀入了隧道下面的大海。

巨石被掀掉了，但是仍然有许多事情要做。隧道顶部必须清理干净，这又花费了两天时间。终于，在2月16日那天营救人员挖到了那辆小汽

---

topple *v.* 倒塌；倒下　　　　　　　　　　　　retrieve *v.* 取回；索回

car. It had taken a direct hit. The force of the falling boulder was so *enormous* it drove the car into the ground. The driver, a 20-year-old clerk, was found dead at the wheel.

The day after that, rescuers finally reached the bus. It, too, had taken a direct hit. The bus had been crushed to a height of just three feet. No one inside was alive. Family members took some comfort in learning that the passengers had died right away. In that sense, the delay in digging out the tunnel had not mattered.

Villagers from Furubira later put up an altar at the tunnel. It was meant to honor the dead. But it also served as a warning. A sign that reads Falling Rocks should be taken seriously. While the odds against it are great, rocks *perched* high above the road can break loose and kill people.

车。落石直接砸在了它上面，巨大的力量竟然把小汽车砸进了地里。而那位司机，一位20岁左右的职员，就死在了方向盘上。

又过了一天，营救人员才清理到公共汽车。它也受到了直接的冲击，被砸得只有三英尺高了，而车里面的人也是无一生还。遇难者的家属得知自己的亲人一定是当场身亡的，他们多少还是得到了少许的安慰——由此看来，挖隧道耽搁时间已经是无关紧要的了。

古平町的村民后来在隧道那里建了一座祭坛，用来纪念死者，同时也是对后来人的警告。隧道边上还设立了一块路标：小心落石。看来被落石砸中的概率还是很大的，公路上方的岩石随时会破土而出然后伤及下面的行人。

---

enormous *adj.* 巨大的　　　　　　　　　　perch *v.* 置于（顶上或边上）

2

A Graveyard Mystery

Harry Spitz seemed like an ordinary little boy. He had his father's looks, with blond hair and brown eyes. He liked to laugh and play with his toys. But was Harry really just an *ordinary* child? That's the question people began to ask in July 1975. By then, Harry had been dead for 63 years. But something

Harry Spitz's grave, shown here as it looks today, is located next to his parents' graves. Harry's vault popped out of the ground on this same spot in 1975.

墓地奇谈
—— 不朽的哈里·斯皮茨

　　哈里·斯皮茨坟墓今天的样子。哈里·斯皮茨的坟墓安置在父母的坟墓旁边，1975年的时候，地下的墓室就拱出了地面。

　　哈里·斯皮茨看起来就是一个普普通通的小男孩。他拥有和他爸爸一样的金色头发，褐色的眼睛。他很喜欢笑，也喜欢玩具。但是哈里真的就是一个普通的孩子吗？这是人们从1975年开始提出的问题。到1975年的时候，哈里已经死了63年了。但是就是在那一年发生的事情，让每个人又

ordinary *adj.* 普通的

happened that summer that made everyone remember him. It made them think perhaps there was more to the little boy than met the eye.

Harry Spitz was born in 1909. He lived with his parents in Morgantown, West Virginia. There his father worked in a glass factory. The family did not have a lot of money. Still, by all accounts, Harry was a happy child. When he was three years old, though, tragedy struck. Harry came down with *cholera*, a deadly disease. Eight days after catching the disease, he died.

Harry's parents were crushed. With heavy hearts they made arrangements for the funeral. His body was dressed in a blue and white *outfit*. Flowers were placed in his hands. His favorite toy—a little stuffed lion—was put into the *casket* with him. The Spitzes had two engraved *plaques* made for the casket. Each read Our Darling.

重新想起了他，人们觉得在这个小男孩身上还有许多不为人知的秘密。

哈里·斯皮茨生于1909年，和他父母一起生活在西弗吉尼亚的摩根城。他的爸爸在一家玻璃厂工作，尽管家境不是很富裕，但是据说哈里是一个快乐的孩子。然而当他三岁的时候悲剧降临了，哈里染上霍乱——一种致命的疾病，患病八天以后，他就死掉了。

哈里的父母都要崩溃了。他们怀着沉痛的心情筹办了葬礼，哈里的遗体穿上了一身蓝白相间的外套；手里握着花；他最喜欢的玩具——一只填充的玩具狮子——也被随身放进了棺材里。斯皮茨夫妇又让人为棺材刻上了两块饰板，每块上面都写着"我们亲爱的孩子"。一块放在了棺材里

cholera *n.* 霍乱　　　　　　　　　　　outfit *n.* 全套服装
casket *n.* 棺材　　　　　　　　　　　plaque *n.* 饰板

One went inside the casket. The second one was set on top.

Many of Harry's playmates came to the funeral. Afterwards a horse-drawn carriage took the casket to Oak Grove Cemetery. There an open grave lay waiting. Several feet down was a concrete *vault*. The casket was lowered into the vault. The *engraved* plaque was placed on top of the casket. Someone laid a single flower on it. Then workers *sealed* the vault with a three-inch-thick concrete lid. They shoveled several feet of dirt on top of the vault to fill up the grave.

Everyone thought that was the end of Harry Spitz. And for 63 years, it was. But on July 2, 1975, Harry was back in the news. That morning the caretaker of Oak Grove Cemetery saw a small pile of dirt near Harry's tombstone. Walking closer, he saw a *bizarre* sight.

面，一块放在了棺材上面。

哈里的很多玩伴都来参加了葬礼，之后，一辆四轮马车把棺材运送到了橡树林公墓。那里已经给小哈里准备好了一穴打开的墓地——一座位于地下几英尺混凝土制成的墓室。棺材就下放到墓室里，雕刻好的金属饰板被安置到了棺材上面，还有人在上面放了一枝花。然后工人们用三英尺厚的混凝土封住了墓室，并且在顶上铲上了几英尺厚的土来填满墓地。

每个人都以为哈里·斯皮茨的一生就这样结束了。但是63年后的1975年7月2日，哈里又回到了公众的视线当中。那天早晨橡树林墓地的看守人发现哈里的墓碑附近出现一小堆土。他走到近前发现了怪异的一幕——哈里墓室上方的土层已经被推到一边，而本来埋在地下的墓室穿透

---

vault *n.* （坟地的）墓穴

seal *v.* 封盖……的表面

engrave *v.* 在……上雕刻（字或图案）

bizarre *adj.* 怪诞的

The ground over Harry's grave had *buckled*. The burial vault was poking up through the grass. The caretaker could see that a corner of the vault had split open, and the lid was resting at an angle. It didn't look like someone had dug up the vault. All the earth had been pushed up from underneath the ground.

The caretaker wasn't sure what to think. He wondered if some kids had set off fireworks near the grave. Perhaps one backfired and *ruptured* the grave. In any case, he called the police. Chief Bennie Palmer and Officer Ralph Chapman took the call. Before seeing the grave, Palmer thought he knew what had happened. From time to time a strange group of people gathered in the cemetery. They tried to make contact with the spirits of dead people. He figured the

草坪露了出来。看守人还发现墓室的一角已经裂开，墓室的盖子错开了一定的角度搭在上面。看起来并不像是有人挖出了墓室，整个土堆是从地下被推上来的。

看守人对自己的考虑没有把握。他想知道是否是孩子在墓地附近放了烟花爆竹，也许是一枚爆竹炸裂了哈里的墓室。但是不管怎样，他还是给警察打了电话。警长本尼·帕尔默和警官拉尔夫·查普曼接的电话。审查墓地之前，帕尔默认为他知道是怎么一回事，有一群陌生人不时地聚集在公墓附近，他们试图和死人的灵魂进行接触。所以帕尔默警官猜测他们那

buckle *v.* （被）压垮；压弯　　　　rupture *v.* （使容器或管道等）破裂

group had come again in the night. He suspected they had set off some kind of explosive device.

When Palmer checked out Harry's grave, however, he changed his mind. "There was no evidence of such a device," he said. In fact, there was no sign of an explosion at all. "We didn't find any evidence of *charred* earth or gunpowder *residues*."

Next Palmer wondered if there was a natural gas leak in the area. Perhaps that could have blown the vault up out of the ground. He called the gas company and asked them to check. Workers did check, but found no leaks.

Palmer and Chapman could not think of anything else that would have caused the vault to pop out of the ground. Yet that's what it

---

天晚上又来了并且怀疑他们安装了某种爆炸装置。

然而，当帕尔默警官检查哈里的坟墓时，他改变了自己的看法。事实上，根本没有迹象显示附近有爆炸发生。"没有证据表明有人使用了这样的装置，"他说，"我们找不到任何烧焦的泥土或者火药残留物的证据。"

接下来帕尔默警官想知道这一地区是否有天然气泄漏，也许会将地下的墓室炸出地面。他给煤气公司打电话要求他们来核查一下，煤气工人检查过后没有发现泄漏。

帕尔默和查普曼想不出其他的任何东西能够使地下的墓室露出地面，可是墓室确实已经露了出来。很明显没有人挖过墓地，也没有任何地方能

---

charred *adj.* 烧焦的　　　　　　　　　　　residue *n.* 残留物

had done. Clearly no one had dug up the grave. There was not a single spot where anything had cut into the ground. "It was a real mystery," Chapman said. "There just weren't any signs of tampering from the outside."

For the next few days many people tried to figure out what had caused Harry Spitz's grave to open. Scientists and professors were consulted. None of them had any answers. There had been no earthquakes or *tremors* in the region. There had been no build-up of gases in the ground or in the vault. As Chief Palmer said, "It was really *baffling*."

At last officials decided to open the vault and take out the casket. Harry's body needed to be reburied anyway. When the *lid* was

---

够让东西插入土里。"这真是一个谜,"查普曼说,"墓穴外没有任何动过的痕迹。"

随后的几天里许多人都试图找出哈里·斯皮茨坟墓开裂的原因。人们咨询了科学家和教授,但是他们也是不明就里。这一地区没有发生过地震,哪怕是轻微的震动;地下或者墓室里也没有天然气的聚集。正如帕尔默警长说的"这一切真让人感到莫名其妙。"

最后警官们决定打开墓室取出棺椁,无论怎样,哈里的尸体需要重新安葬。当墓室的拱顶被搬开时,神秘的气息变得浓重起来,那块雕刻的金

---

tremor *n.* 微震   baffling *adj.* 令人困惑的
lid *n.* 盖子

removed from the vault, the mystery just got deeper. The engraved plaque was still perched on top of the rounded casket. So was the single dried flower. This meant no explosion could possibly have pushed the vault up through the ground. Anything that shook the vault that much would have caused the plaque and flower to fall off.

The case was already an *eerie* one. But it got even *spookier* when workers opened the casket. Harry's body was indeed lying inside. But it did not look like it had been there for 63 years. "The body ... was not in the bare-bones state, which it should have been after all that time," said Chapman. Everyone had expected to see little more than a *skeleton*. Instead, they saw a little boy who looked like he was sleeping. His hands still held a *bouquet* of dried flowers. "The body

---

属饰板仍然安置在圆顶的棺木盖子上，甚至那支已经枯萎的花朵也没有改变位置。这就意味着不是爆炸把墓室推上地面的，因为任何能够使墓室上升的震动都会让金属饰板和花从棺椁上跌落下来。

事件到此已经谜团不解，但是当工作人员打开棺材的时候，里面的景象更是让他们感到毛骨悚然。哈里的尸体确实躺在棺材内，但是看起来并不像已经安放了63年的样子。查普曼说："尸体……并不是一具骨头架子，而经历了这么长的时间肉本应该都烂掉了。"人们都以为他们将看到的是一具骷髅，但是实际上呈现在他们眼前的是一个仿佛正在熟睡的小男孩，他的手里还握着一束已经枯萎的花朵。孩子的皮肤有些类似皮革般的弹性，但是小哈里的尸体依然保持着令人难以置信的状态。查普曼说道：

---

eerie *adj.* 神秘的
skeleton *n.* 骨骼

spooky *adj.* 令人毛骨悚然的
bouquet *n.* 花束

still had *intact* skin," said Chapman. That skin was a little *leathery*, but everything else about Harry was in remarkably good shape. "He even had lots of long blond hair."

No one could explain it. But many people were a bit frightened by it. They wondered what it all meant. They wondered what forces had been at work in the grave. And they wished they knew more about the little boy who was buried there.

On July 12, 1975, Harry Spitz's body was buried for a second time. His casket was put into a new, sealed vault. Since then the vault has remained where it belongs—deep in the ground. But no one knows how much longer it will stay that way.

"尸体的皮肤完好无损，他甚至还有许多金色的长发。"

没有人能够解释这一切，但是许多人都害怕了。他们想知道这究竟意味着什么，他们也想知道是什么力量在墓穴中发挥了作用。他们多么希望对埋在这里的小男孩能有更多的了解啊！

1975年7月12日人们又一次安葬了哈里·斯皮茨。他的棺椁被安放进了一座新的、密封的墓穴里。从那时候起墓室就一直安放在本就属于它的地方——地下深处。但是没有人知道它会在那里待上多长时间。

---

intact *adj.* 完好无损的   leathery *adj.* 似皮革的

The Money Pit

In the year 1795, a teenager named Dan McGinnis *paddled* his canoe to *Oak* Island. At that time no one lived on the small island off the coast of Nova Scotia. So it was a fine spot for a young boy to hunt. But McGinnis did not do much hunting that day. Instead, he found something that has

This photograph of the Money Pit was taken in 1955 during one of the many unsuccessful attempts to reach the bottom.

宝藏诱惑
——橡树岛的钱坑

这张钱坑照片于1995年拍摄，照片中的工人们正在进行着到达坑底的努力，这仅仅是许多失败尝试中的又一次而已。

1795年，一个名叫丹·麦克金尼斯的少年划着他的独木舟来到了橡树岛。那个时候，在这座远离加拿大新斯科舍省海岸的小岛上并没有人居住，因此这是一个青少年狩猎的好去处。但是那天麦克金尼斯并没有过多狩猎。相反，他发现了些事情，从那以后这些事情便一直困扰着加拿大人。

paddle *v.* 用桨划船

oak *n.* 橡树

puzzled the people of Canada ever since.

While resting under a tree, McGinnis saw a round depression in the ground. He also spotted a *notch* in one of the tree's branches. It looked as if the branch had been used as part of a *pulley*. McGinnis's mind began to race. He had heard tales of *pirates* in the region. Had pirates buried treasure under this tree?

The next day McGinnis returned to the island with two friends. They began to dig. The boys dug only a few feet when they hit something hard. It was a layer of flagstones. There was something buried here!

The boys dug faster and faster. At 10 feet they ran into a layer of wooden *planks*. They hoped that there was treasure buried under the planks, but there wasn't. There was just more dirt. Still, they

---

在一棵树下休息的时候，麦克金尼斯看到地上有一片圆形塌陷的痕迹。他又发现旁边树上的枝杈中有一个雕刻过的V字形切口，看起来树杈是被用作滑轮装置的一部分了。麦克金尼斯的大脑开始高速运转，他以前听说过这个地区有海盗的传闻，难道海盗曾经在这棵树下埋藏财宝了吗？

第二天麦克金尼斯和两个朋友又来到了这座岛上，他们开始挖掘。只挖了几英尺深的时候就碰到了硬的东西，那是一层石板，一定有什么东西埋在这儿！

几个小男孩越挖越快，在地下10英尺处他们碰到了一层木板。他们希望有财宝埋藏在木板底下，但是没有，只有很多的淤泥。尽管如此，他

---

notch *n.* V形刻痕；圆形切口

pirate *n.* （尤指旧时的）海盗

pulley *n.* 滑轮

plank *n.* 木板

figured someone had put the planks there for a reason. There had to be treasure somewhere in the pit. They just had to dig deeper.

Day after day the boys returned to the deserted island. At 20 feet, they hit another layer of planks. Excitedly, they lifted them up. But again, all they found was more dirt. They resumed digging.

At 30 feet they hit a third layer of wooden planks. Again, there was nothing *underneath* but more dirt. By this time winter was coming. The boys couldn't dig any more. But they *vowed* to return to the island in the future and uncover the treasure. They were sure something important was buried there. Why else would anyone have built such an *elaborate* pit?

The boys dug on and off for the next few years without reaching the bottom of the *pit*. They grew to be adults. Still, they dreamed of

---

们推测这里有木板一定是有原因的，坑里面的某个地方一定有财宝，他们只好往更深的地方挖下去。

孩子们日复一日地返回这座荒凉的小岛。在地下20英尺处他们又遇到了一层木板。孩子们异常兴奋地把木板抬了出来，但再一次，他们发现的是更多的污泥，他们又恢复了挖掘工作。

在挖到地下30英尺的时候他们遇到了第三块木板，然而地下除了淤泥还是什么都没有。那时候冬天已经来临了，孩子们不能再继续挖掘，但是他们发誓将来要重返小岛取出财宝。他们确信一定有某些重要的东西埋在那里，否则还有什么其他原因能让人建造一个如此复杂精致的坑呢？

孩子们断断续续地挖了几年，但是都没有挖到坑底。那时候他们都已长

---

underneath *adv.* 在下面；在底下
elaborate *adj.* 复杂的；精心制作的

vow *v.* 发誓
pit *n.* 深坑

finding treasure in what became known as the Money Pit. In 1804 they joined a company formed *solely* to find the treasure. With better tools, they could now dig deeper.

But even with the new tools, it was the same story all over again. Every 10 feet, the workers hit a layer of oak planks. Under every layer of planks there was more dirt. They did get a few *thrills*, however. At 40 feet they found a layer of *charcoal* on top of the planks. At 50 feet there was a layer of *putty* like the kind used to seal ships. Ten more feet, and they dug up coconut fibers. At last, at 90 feet, they found a stone marked with strange writing.

They began to get excited when they found the stone. This had to be it! The next day the workers returned, brimming with hope. But one look down into the Money Pit deflated all their dreams. The pit

---

大成人却仍然梦想着在那块被称作"钱坑"的地方找到财宝。1804年他们加入了一个专门为寻宝而成立的公司，有了更好的工具他们可以挖得更深。

　　但即使运用了全新的工具，他们依然重复着相同的经历。每向下挖10英尺，工人们就会碰到一层橡木板，每层橡木板下只有更多的淤泥。然而他们确实也有激动的时候，在40英尺处他们在木板上方发现了一层木炭；在50英尺处，有一层像是用来封船用的胶泥；再往下挖10英尺，他们挖出了椰子纤维。最后在地下90英尺的地方他们发现了一块刻有奇怪文字的石头。

　　当他们发现石头的时候，他们开始兴奋起来，宝藏一定就是它。可是第二天工人们满怀希望返回来的时候，眼前的一切打碎了他们所有的梦

---

solely *adv.* 只；惟

charcoal *n.* 木炭

thrill *n.* 激动；兴奋

putty *n.* （窗用）油灰

had flooded overnight. It was filled with water all the way up to the 33-foot level. No amount of *bailing* with buckets or pumping could empty the pit.

As it turned out, this was a *booby trap*. Whoever built the Money Pit wanted to keep outsiders away. So a tunnel had been created that led from the pit to the ocean. The digging had opened that tunnel. That meant that water flowed freely from the ocean into the pit.

McGinnis and his friends were *frustrated*. But they weren't ready to give up yet. If they couldn't dig any further into the Money Pit, they reasoned, then they would dig a second pit right next to it. When they were deep enough, they would cut over to the Money Pit and grab the treasure.

想——深坑一夜之间涨满了水。水一直涨到33英尺处，即使用桶舀或者用水泵抽也无法排空。

原来这是一个陷阱，设计钱坑的人想把外来者拒之门外，因此设计者开了一条隧道直通大海。现在挖掘打通了那条隧道，这就意味着水可以从海洋中自由地灌入坑内。

麦克金尼斯和朋友们感到很沮丧，但是他们并没有打算放弃。他们推断现在的坑已经无法再继续向下挖了，如果在旁边再挖一个坑洞，当新坑足够深的时候，横向穿进第一座坑里，就一定会得到财宝。

---

bail v. （从……中）往外舀水   booby trap 饵雷；陷阱
frustrated adj. 令人沮丧的；令人灰心的

The workers dug a 110-foot shaft. But when they started to cut over, water rushed into the new *shaft* as well. They had to *scramble* to escape with their lives. Soon the second shaft had just as much water in it as the Money Pit. All McGinnis and the others had to show for their work was two holes filled with water.

For years after that, the Money Pit lay untouched. But in 1849 a new group came to the island. Calling themselves the Truro Company, they vowed to solve the mystery. They brought in the most up-to-date mining equipment they could find. Then they drilled down and collected *samples* of whatever lay at the bottom of the pit. They came up with pieces of oak, *spruce*, and metal. These clues suggested the drill had hit chests filled with coins. They also found three small gold links from a chain. But there was no way to get at

---

工人们于是又挖了一条110英尺深的矿井般的地洞。但是当他们准备横向穿进原来的坑洞的时候，水涌入了新挖的坑里面。他们不得不争先爬出洞口逃命。瞬间第二口坑和旁边的那个一样也积满了水。这就是麦克金尼斯和其他人的工作成果，两个灌满水的地洞。

从那以后若干年没有人再来碰过这座钱坑，直到1849年又有一伙人来到了岛上。这伙人自称初罗公司，发誓要解开这个秘密。他们带来了当时能找到的最新式的开矿工具，然后就开始工作。他们把在坑底能够找到的一切样本都收集起来，发现了一些橡树、云杉或者金属的碎屑，这些线索表明钻头已经碰到了装满钱币的箱子。他们也找到了三枚链子上的小金

---

shaft *n.* 通道
sample *n.* 样本

scramble *v.* 争夺
spruce *n.* 云杉

the treasure. No matter what they did, water always filled the pit.

Over the years other people have tried their luck. Some have built more shafts. (In fact, people have built so many shafts that no one now knows which one is the *original* Money Pit.) They have built *dams* to try to stop the flooding. They have tried better pumps. But nothing has worked. No one has ever found any coins or gold.

Millions of dollars have been spent trying to find the treasure. There have been human costs as well. Treasure hunters have been killed in the Money Pit. One man died when a water boiler blew up. Another fell to his death while being pulled up from the bottom of the pit. In 1965, a father, his son, and two friends drowned in the pit.

The Money Pit has remained a mystery for over 200 years. To this day, no one knows if there is treasure buried there, or why such an

---

环，但是他们能得到的就是这么多了。无论他们做什么，水总是把坑洞填得满满的。

多年以来，其他人也来碰过运气，他们挖了许多坑。（实际上人们已经挖了很多坑，没有人知道哪一个是最初的那个了。）建造水坝阻挡洪流，也尝试过更好的水泵，但是没有奏效，没有人发现任何的钱币或黄金。

寻宝花掉了数百万美元，同时也付出了生命的代价。许多寻宝人死在了钱坑之中，一个人被爆炸的锅炉炸死；另一位在从坑底向上拉的过程中摔死；1965年，一位父亲和儿子及两个朋友在坑中淹死。

200多年过去了，钱坑依然是一个谜。直到今天也没有人知道是否有财宝埋在那里，最初为什么建立这样一座精致的坑。但是还有另一个谜

---

original *adj.* 最初的   dam *n.* 水坝

elaborate pit was built in the first place. But there is another mystery, as well: Who built the pit? Dan McGinnis thought the builders were pirates. But that is not likely. Whoever built the pit had to be an engineer with a team of skilled miners. No known *pirate* had the skill or support to *construct* such a pit.

Rupert Furneaux, author of *The Money Pit Mystery*, may have a better answer. He thinks gold was buried on Oak Island during the American Revolution. The British governor of New York had the gold to pay all of the British forces in America. In 1778 it looked like the Americans might *capture* New York City. So perhaps the governor sent the money to Nova Scotia to be buried. The British army would have had the right skills to build the pit.

团：谁建造了这个坑？丹·麦克金尼斯认为建造者是海盗，但那是不可能的。任何能建造这样一座坑的人都必须拥有一个工程师和一个有技术矿工队，已知的海盗中没有人能够具有这样的技术或者承担得起建坑的费用。

《钱坑之谜》的作者鲁珀特·菲尔诺也许会有更好的答案。他认为金子是在美国大革命时期埋在橡树岛的，当时驻扎在纽约的英国统治者就用这笔黄金来支付英国军队在美国的费用。1778年的时候，美国人看起来要攻克纽约城了，因此总督派人把钱送往新斯科舍埋藏起来。英国军队应该有正确的技术建造这样的坑。

---

pirate *n.* 海盗

capture *v.* 占领

construct *v.* 建造

There is a problem with this theory, however. There is no record that the British lost a huge sum of money during that time. Furneaux thinks he can explain that too. He believes the British dug up the money themselves soon after hiding it. He thinks the pit is just that—a pit.

Maybe Furneaux is right. Maybe there is nothing in the Money Pit but water and broken dreams. On the other hand, no one has explained how the British could have gotten the *treasure* out of the pit. And no one has explained why bits of gold, metal, and wood would still be in the bottom of the pit. So maybe there are chests of gold down there. Maybe they are just waiting for someone to pull them out. Could that someone be you?

　　然而这个理论也存在问题，因为那段时间并没有英国人丢失大批钱财的记录。菲尔诺认为他可以解释这个质疑，他相信英军在埋了以后很快又自己挖出了钱财。他认为坑就是当年那个埋钱的坑。

　　也许菲尔诺是对的，也许除了水和破灭的梦想之外钱坑里面什么都没有。另一方面，没有人能解释出英国人是如何把钱取出来的；也没有人能解释为什么在坑底依然存有黄金、金属和木头碎屑。因此，也许那里还存放着一箱箱的黄金，也许这些黄金正在等着某人去让它们重见天日，那个人会是你吗？

---

treasure *n.* 金银财宝；财富

The Man-Eaters of Tsavo

These days they're harmless. In fact, you can find them *mounted* and on display at Chicago's Field Museum. But when they were alive, they were a *terror*. There were only two of them, but they killed at will. People lost sleep worrying about who would be the next victim. One person died of shock just thinking

Today the lions that plagued the Tsavo area are mounted and on exhibit at Chicago's Field Museum. They killed more than 120 people while they were alive.

谈狮色变
——沙窝的食人魔

曾经在沙窝为害一方的狮子如今被陈列在芝加哥田园博物馆内，它们活着的时候咬死了120多个人。

现在它们不能再为非作歹了，你可以在芝加哥田园博物馆里看到它们的标本。可是当年活着的时候，它们却是恐怖主义者。虽然只有两头，但是它们却可以恣意妄为地杀人，人们由于担心成为下一个受害者而整夜失

mounted *adj.* 安装好的；配有承载物的　　　　terror *n.* 可怕的人；恐怖的事

about "the man-eaters of Tsavo."

In 1898 the British were building a railroad across east Africa. It was not an easy task. The tracks crossed mile after mile of *barren* land. Food, water, and supplies had to be *hauled* in from far away. Skilled workers had to be brought in from the East Indies. Then, when the railroad workers reached the Tsavo River, they faced an even bigger problem. This new problem was lions— two huge lions that fed on human flesh.

Colonel John Henry Patterson was in charge of the railroad project. At first he didn't believe the workers' stories of lion attacks. He thought they were just rumors. Then one night he became *convinced* of the lions' existence. One of the lions *snuck* into the tent of a railroad worker. The lion grabbed the worker by the throat.

眠，甚至有一个人因为想到"沙窝的食人魔"而被吓死。

1898年英国人兴建一条横跨东非的铁路。那并不是一个简单的任务，铁轨需要一英里一英里地穿过贫瘠的土地；食品、水以及补给品都需要从远方运来；技术工人也都是从东印度公司招募的。然而当筑路工人到达沙窝河时，他们面临着一个更严峻的问题，这个新问题就是狮子——两头以人肉为食的大狮子。

铁路工程的负责人是约翰·亨利·帕特森上校。起初他并不相信狮子袭击工人的说法，认为那只是谣言。后来的一天晚上他开始相信了狮子的存在，因为一头狮子潜进了一个铁路工人的帐篷，咬住了一名工人的喉

---

barren *adj.* 贫瘠的

convinced *adj.* 确信的；信服的

haul *v.* 拖运

sneak *v.* 潜行

As another worker watched in horror, he was dragged out of the tent. "Let go!" he cried. But the lion's *grip* was too strong. The next day, Patterson found the worker's remains. It was not a pretty sight.

The other workers, of course, were terrified. Many ran away or refused to work. Patterson was scared too. He also knew that the lions had to be killed. Otherwise, the railroad line would never get finished. Being a skilled hunter, he decided that he would kill them himself. He didn't think it would be that hard to do. He was wrong.

That night Patterson, taking his *rifle*, climbed up into a tree near the area where the worker had been killed. There he waited for the lions. He had tied a goat to the tree, hoping this tasty meal would *entice* them. The lions, however, had a different meal in mind. Late that night, one of the cats attacked another tent, far away from

---

啦。当另一名工人惊恐万状地看着眼前的景象时，狮子把他拖出了帐篷，他拼命喊道："放开我！"但是狮子实在是太强大了。第二天，帕特森发现了那名工人的残骸，当时的情景惨不忍睹。

当然，其他的工人也吓坏了，许多人都吓跑了或者拒绝再工作。帕特森也感到很恐惧，他也知道必须除掉狮子，否则铁路线就不会完工。作为一名有经验的猎手，他决定亲自收拾他们，帕特森上校认为这并不会太难办，但是他错了。

那天晚上，帕特森带上猎枪，爬到了距离工人被害地点不远的一棵树上，在那里"守株待狮"。树下系了一只山羊，上校希望这顿可口的晚餐可以成为狮子的诱饵。然而，狮子的心中自有一顿不同的美餐。那天深夜，一只

---

grip *n.* 紧咬

entice *v.* 引诱

rifle *n.* 步枪

the spot where Patterson was waiting, and dragged away another worker.

Patterson heard the victim's screams, but there was little he could do. Work camps *stretched* for eight miles along the railroad. He couldn't guard them all. Instead, he decided to build thick thorn *fences* around each camp. He thought that would keep the man-eaters out. The workers felt much safer with the fences in place. They also began keeping a fire burning in each camp throughout the night.

None of these safety measures worked, however. The lions never missed a meal. They either jumped over the fences or they *crawled* through weak spots in them. Once again, the killings *terrorized* the workers.

狮子袭击了离帕特森守候地很远的一处营房并且又拖走了一名工人。

当时帕特森听到了受害者的惊叫，但是他也无能为力。工人的帐篷顺着铁路线绵延了8英里，他不可能为所有的帐篷担任警戒。作为补救措施，他决定在每个帐篷前建起带粗刺的篱笆，认为这会把吃人者挡在外面。有了篱笆挡在那里，工人们也觉得安全多了，而且他们还在每座帐篷外面通宵燃起篝火。

然而这所有的一切防护措施都变成了摆设，狮子从来没有耽误过自己的美餐。他们要么跃过篱笆要么从有漏洞的地方钻过去，杀戮再一次使工人们惶恐不安起来。

---

stretch *v.* 延续；连绵

crawl *v.* 爬行

fence *n.* 篱笆

terrorize *v.* 使恐怖

Patterson was frightened, too. "In the whole of my life," he said, "I have never experienced anything more nerve shaking than to hear the deep roars of these dreadful monsters." When the roaring came closer, "[I knew] that some one or other of us was *doomed* to be their victim." Just before the lions entered a camp, their roaring ceased. That's when the men knew one of the lions was stalking its prey. Soon the beast would attack. But where? Patterson never seemed to guess right. He kept setting traps, but the lions kept striking someplace else. The lions, he later said, always seemed to know where his traps were.

At last, Patterson decided to try a new *tactic*. He would no longer wait for the lions to come to him. He would hunt the lions on their own ground. Day after day he crawled through the bushes. He never

---

帕特森也害怕了。"在我的一生中，"他说，"我从来没有过比听到这可怕怪物深沉的吼声更为恐怖的声音。"当吼声接近时，"我知道我们当中的某个人注定要成为牺牲品。"就在狮子进入帐篷之前，吼叫声停止了。人们知道那是狮子正在偷偷地接近猎物，瞬间这头猛兽就要发动进攻，但是它在哪里？帕特森从来没有猜对过。他不断地设陷阱，但狮子一次次地攻击别的地方。后来他说，狮子好像总是知道陷阱在哪里。

最后，帕特森决定尝试新的策略。他不再等着狮子送上门来，而是主动出击去搜寻它们。他日复一日地爬过灌木林，但总是一无所获。这也许

---

doom *v.* 注定

tactic *n.* 策略

found them. That was probably just as well. If he had come across them, they would almost certainly have killed him before he could kill them.

Meanwhile, work on the railroad had come to a complete stop. Hundreds of workers had run away. Those who stayed could think of only one thing—how to stay safe. Some tied their beds up in trees. Others slept on the top of water tanks or roofs. Still others stayed in their tents but dug *pits* in the middle of the dirt floor. They slept in the pits, which they covered over with heavy *logs*.

One day Patterson came across a donkey that the lions had killed. They hadn't eaten all of it and Patterson thought they might return to finish their meal. So he built a platform near the donkey's body outside one of the camps. That night he sat on the top of the

---

不必遗憾，如果他真的遇到了狮子，可能在开枪之前就已经被咬死了。

与此同时，修建铁路的工作已经完全停了下来。数百名工人都跑掉了，那些留下来的人也只是在考虑一件事情——怎样才能保住性命。有些人把床拴在了树上；其他人则睡在了水箱或者房屋顶上；还有些人依旧睡在帐篷里，但是在泥地中间挖了个坑，他们睡在坑内，上面盖上了重重的缘木。

一天帕特森遇到一头被狮子猎杀的死驴。它们还没有吃完这头驴子，帕特森想狮子可能会再回来吃光这顿晚餐的。因此他在营房外面靠近死驴处搭建了一座平台，那天晚上他手持步枪在平台顶上等候着狮子的到来。

---

pit *n.* 洼坑

log *n.* 原木

platform with his rifle and waited.

Soon one of the lions came near. With no moon, the night was black, and it was difficult to see. But Patterson could hear the lion's deep sigh. The animal was hungry. But it was not going after the donkey. It was going after Patterson! Slowly the lion circled the platform. Patterson sat there terrified, "hardly daring even to *blink* my eyes."

The lion came closer and closer. Still Patterson could not see it. Then at last he saw the lion's *faint* form crouched under a nearby bush. Patterson pulled the *trigger* of his rifle. The lion gave a terrific roar. It ran into the thick brush. Patterson kept firing where he thought the lion was hiding. The lion's *growls* turned to moans. Then the night was silent. One of the man-eaters of Tsavo was dead.

不久，一只狮子出现了。当时夜色漆黑，连月亮也躲了起来，很难看清眼前的动静。帕特森可以听到这头狮子深深的喘息声。这个家伙很饥饿，但是它并没有碰那头死驴，而是向帕特森奔了过来，缓缓地绕着平台转。帕特森惊恐地坐在那里，甚至都不敢眨一下眼睛。

狮子越来越近了，帕特森却还是看不清楚它。终于，他发现了狮子模糊的轮廓蹲伏在附近一丛灌木中，帕特森扣动了步枪的扳机。狮子发出了可怖的哀号，随后向丛林深处跑去。帕特森连续向狮子逃跑的方向射击，狮子的吼叫变成了呻吟。而后，夜寂静了下来，一头"沙窝食人魔"被击毙了。

---

blink *v.* 眨眼睛
trigger *n.* （枪炮的）扳机

faint *adj.* 模糊的
growl *n.* 怒吼声

The shooting woke up the whole camp. When the workers heard the news they gave a loud cheer. "Every man in camp came out," said Patterson, "tom toms split the night air and *horns* were blown as men came running to the scene." The workers danced the rest of the night away.

The dead lion was huge. It measured nearly nine feet in length and three and a half feet in height. (Male lions rarely grow more than eight feet in length and three feet in height.) It took eight men to carry its body to camp.

One lion was dead, but there was still one roaming free. For the second lion, Patterson used dead goats as *bait*. When the lion approached, he shot it in the shoulder. This lion, however, managed to slip away before he could shoot it again. Ten days later, the beast came back to get one of the men sleeping in a tree. This time

---

　　枪声惊醒了整个营房，工人们听到这个消息发出了极大的欢呼声。"营地的所有人都跑了出来，"帕特森说，"当人们跑到场外时，唐鼓的鼓点和号角声划破了夜空的宁静。"工人们一直跳舞到天亮。

　　死掉的狮子十分庞大，大约有9英尺长3英尺半高。（雄狮很少有长度超过8英尺高度超过3英尺的。）费了8个人的力气才把它的尸体抬到营地。

　　一头狮子死了，但还有一头逍遥法外。对付第二头狮子，帕特森用只死羊作诱饵。当狮子靠近时，他开枪射中了它的肩部，可是狮子在帕特森开第二枪之前就逃走了。10天之后，这头野兽回来捕捉一名睡在树上的

---

horn *n.* 号角

bait *n.* 诱饵

Patterson was in the right place. He fired shots at the lion, but didn't kill it. The next night, Patterson climbed the same tree. When the lion returned, he shot it in the chest. Once again, the lion got away, badly wounded but not dead.

In the morning Patterson went after the lion. He knew it was injured, so he thought it would be easy to hunt it down. He spotted the lion hiding in some bushes. He fired his rifle. He hit the lion, but that didn't stop it from charging. Patterson shot it again and again. Each time the lion tumbled to the ground only to get up and charge once more. Finally, its leg *shattered*, the lion could barely move. Patterson killed it with another volley of shots.

The lions' *reign* of terror was over. The workers returned to their jobs. By then, however, "the man-eaters of Tsavo" had claimed more than 120 lives.

工人，这次它被帕特森逮了一个正着。上校瞄准狮子射击，但是没有打死它。第二天晚上，帕特森爬上同一棵树，当狮子返回来的时候，他一枪击中了这头野兽的胸部。狮子再一次带着重伤逃走了，但是它仍然没有死掉。

第二天清晨帕特森去追踪狮子，他知道狮子受了伤，因此很容易捕获。他在一处灌木丛里发现了狮子，于是向它开火。子弹击中了它，但是并没有阻挡住这个家伙。兽性大发的狮子每一次跌倒后都爬起来进行又一次的反扑。终于，狮子的腿被击中，它再也无法进行回击了，帕特森在它身上又射了一梭子子弹。

狮子的恐怖统治结束了，工人们又恢复了工作。然而到那时候为止，据称这两个"沙窝的食人魔"已经伤害了120条人命。

---

shatter *v.* 碎裂；破碎   reign *n.* 统治

5

The Evil Eye

Bad luck seemed to follow Spain's King Alfonso. In 1923, he sailed to Italy. Some Italians rowed out to greet him. As they *approached* the king, a wave hit their boat. Several men were washed overboard and *drowned*. The Italians tried to continue with their

In many countries the image of an eye is often painted on the front of a boat. Some people believe that this keeps the boat safe from the curse of the evil eye.

致命一瞥
——邪恶目光的传说

许多国家，人们都在船头画上眼睛的形象。有些人相信这样可以保护船只避免邪恶眼神的诅咒。

霉运似乎总跟着阿方索。1923年，这位西班牙国王乘船去意大利访问，一些意大利人列队出来欢迎。当他们就要靠近国王的时候，一个大浪拍在了他们的船上，几个人被打落到水中淹死了。意大利人继续他们的欢迎活动，

---

approach v. 接近；靠近　　　　　　　　　　drown v. 淹死；溺死

welcome. One boat fired a *cannon* in Alfonso's honor. The cannon blew up, killing the crew. Next a *naval* officer shook the king's hand. A short time later the officer dropped dead.

Finally, the Italians took the king on a tour around a local lake. But during the tour the lake's dam burst. Fifty people drowned. Hundreds of others saw their homes washed away before their eyes.

Was it just *coincidence*? Benito Mussolini, the leader of Italy at that time, didn't think so. He refused to meet with Alfonso. Instead, he sent an advisor to meet with him. Mussolini stayed away from Alfonso because he was sure the king had the evil eye. Mussolini did not want that deadly eye turned on him.

Belief in the evil eye is very old. It is often brought up when things

出于对阿方索的敬意，一只船点燃了大炮，可是大炮爆炸炸死了船员。接下来一位海军军官与国王握手，然而不久以后这位军官暴毙身亡。

最后，意大利人带领国王游览当地的一个湖泊，在观光期间湖坝突然决堤，淹死了50个人。其余的数百人眼睁睁地看着他们的同胞被水冲走。

难道这仅仅是巧合吗？当时的意大利元首本尼托·墨索里尼却不这么认为。他拒绝会晤阿方索，而是派一名顾问代他去迎接。墨索里尼避开阿方索，是因为他相信国王有双凶眼，墨索里尼可不想那致命的目光落到他的身上。

人们从很久以前就开始相信邪恶目光的传说，每当事情出现了异常他

cannon *n.* 大炮   naval *adj.* 海军的
coincidence *n.* 巧合

go wrong. People have blamed the evil eye for crop failures. They have used it to explain the sickness of animals. They have even said the evil eye causes death. One ancient Jewish book issued this dire warning: "For every [person] that dies of natural causes, ninety-nine will die of the evil eye."

What exactly is the evil eye? Believers say it is a powerful look that can be given at any time. The one who gives it might be trying to *curse* you. On the other hand, he or she might not be aware of what is happening. Either way, they say, the person has a dark and dangerous force *dwelling* in his or her soul. When that force is trained on you, trouble is sure to come your way.

Who has the evil eye, according to believers? There are many answers to that question. Often people who look a bit different are

---

们就认为是这个传说引起的。人们把庄稼歉收归咎于邪恶的目光；用它来解释动物生病的原因；他们甚至说邪恶眼神能引起死亡。一本犹太古书发出了这样一条可怕的警告："对于每个自然死亡的人来讲，百分之九十九都将死于邪恶的目光。"

邪恶的目光到底是什么？笃信者说那是随时可以发出富有魔力的一瞥，那一瞥的主人可能正试图诅咒你。另一方面，他或者她也许并没有意识到所发生的一切。笃信者认为，不管哪种情况，那个人的灵魂深处都拥有黑暗而可怕的力量，当那种力量瞄上你的时候，麻烦定要随你而来。

如果这些笃信者的说法是正确的，谁会拥有邪恶的目光呢？这个问题有许多答案。人们通常认为那些看起来有点与众不同的人拥有这样的眼

---

curse v. 诅咒

dwell v. 居住；存在于

MCGRAW-HILL

thought to have it. In Turkey, that means people with blue eyes. In parts of Africa it means those with *squinty* eyes. In other places it means someone who is cross-eyed or left-handed or childless.

In the past true believers went to great lengths to protect themselves from the evil eye. The color red was thought to protect against it, so Italian brides often covered their heads with red *veils*. In Scotland farmers tied red *ribbons* to the tails of their *livestock*. In the 17th century even judges were afraid. Some judges made defendants enter the court backwards! That way the defendants couldn't look them in the eye.

Today some people still believe in the evil eye and work hard to avoid it. They wear special charms to keep themselves safe. These charms may be in the shape of an eye or a hand or a horseshoe.

神。在土耳其，他们指的是蓝眼睛的人；在非洲的部分地区，指的是那些斜视的人；在其他地方则指那些有斗鸡眼或者善用左手或者没有子女的人。

过去真正的笃信者不遗余力地防止自身遭受邪恶的目光。人们认为红色可以抵御它，因此在意大利，新娘经常用红纱盖头；在苏格兰，农民们把红带子系到牲畜的尾巴上。甚至17世纪的法官都惧怕邪恶的目光，一些法官让被告倒着进入法庭，这样被告就不能用眼睛看他们了。

如今一些人依然对邪恶的目光深信不疑，并且在努力地避免遇到它。他们佩戴特殊的符咒来保证安全，这些符咒呈眼睛、手或者马蹄状。在希

---

squinty *adj.* 斜视的
ribbon *n.* 缎带；丝带

veil *n.* 面纱
livestock *n.* 牲畜

In Greece and Turkey a blue glass eye charm is used. This eye supposedly acts as a mirror. If the evil eye is thrown at the wearer, the glass eye will *bounce* the evil back in the other direction.

Fishing boats in Europe often have an eye painted on the bow to ward off the evil eye. Garlic and sage are used in some places. In the United States and Canada farmers often nail a horseshoe over their barn doors. In the Middle East some people carry two *marbles* with them at all times. One is black and one is white. The white marble protects them in the daytime. The black marble protects them at night.

Those who believe in the evil eye say that it is most dangerous to babies. So some parents keep their newborn in the house for the

---

腊和土耳其则使用玻璃制的蓝色眼睛符咒，这只眼睛被当作一面镜子，如果邪恶的眼神投射到戴符咒人的身上，玻璃眼睛就会将邪恶反射到另一个方向。

欧洲的渔船常在船头画上一只眼睛以避开邪恶的目光；有些地方使用的是大蒜和鼠尾草；美国和加拿大的农民们常在牲口圈门前钉一块马蹄铁；中东一些人总是携带两块大理石———一块黑色一块白色，天亮的时候白色大理石保护他们，天黑的时候黑色大理石保护他们。

那些笃信者说邪恶目光对婴儿是最危险的，因此有些父母在头一个

---

bounce *v.* 反射   marble *n.* 大理石

first month. Sooner or later, though, they have to take the child out into the world. Here the danger is great. Many people want to look at the baby, but one of them might have the evil eye. Parents live in fear that a stranger will praise their child. They *dread* hearing the words, "Oh, what a pretty baby!" They believe that praise can be a curse sent by someone with the evil eye.

Friends of the parents know how to *compliment* the baby safely. They rub a bit of dirt on the child's clothes. Then they say, "What a pretty baby—too bad she is so dirty." Because they have found something bad to say, the parents know that no curse is being sent.

If the evil eye is given to the baby, parents must act quickly. They must spit on their child. Or they must say something bad about the

---

月里会把新生儿放在屋里。然而他们迟早会把孩子带到外面的世界的，那里有数不清的危险。很多人想看看孩子；但是他们中也许就有眼光邪恶者。父母们生怕陌生人表扬他们的孩子，很担心听到"啊，多漂亮的宝贝呀！"他们相信这些夸赞可能就是某种有邪恶目光的人发出的诅咒。

父母的朋友们知道如何安全地赞扬孩子。他们故意在孩子的衣服上涂抹些泥土，然后说："多俊俏的孩子呀，可惜糟糕的是她太脏了。"因为他们在孩子身上找到了一些毛病，父母知道他们没有发出诅咒。

如果邪恶的目光注视到了孩子，父母必须马上采取行动。他们必须在孩子身上吐上几口，或者必须说些孩子的坏话来取消这个诅咒。

---

dread *v.* 担心　　　　　　　　　　　　compliment *v.* 赞扬

child to cancel out the curse.

There are other ways to break the evil eye curse. One way is to have someone pass a raw egg over the cursed person's face and then break the egg. You could try *piercing* a lemon with nails. If that doesn't work, you should spit at the person with the evil eye three times.

How can you be sure that you don't have the evil eye? You can't. Most of you are probably okay. But just in case, be sure not to *stare* at people. It isn't polite, and besides, you might wind up with a bunch of people spitting back at you!

还有其他方法可以解除邪恶目光的诅咒。一种方法是让人将生鸡蛋滚过受了诅咒的人的脸然后打破鸡蛋；你还可以用钉子刺破一个柠檬，如果不起作用，你应该往那个眼光邪恶的人吐上三口。

你们怎么能知道自己身上没有邪恶的目光呢？你不能知道，大多数人都应该是安全的。但是为了以防万一，一定不要直盯着别人。那样既不礼貌，也有可能会招来一群人向你吐口水。

---

pierce *v.* 刺破

stare *v.* 凝视；盯着看

6

The Rainmaker

San Diego needed rain. Even in a good year, only about 10 inches of rain fall on this California city. But in the late 1800s, that number was way down. *Severe* droughts were hurting the city. If San Diego wanted to grow in size and wealth, it needed water.

Charles Hatfield claimed that the 23 chemicals he mixed together could "make" rain. Here he is mixing the "rain stew" that brought a record 38 inches of rain to the city of San Dieao.

人工求雨
——神奇的降雨先驱

查尔斯·海特菲尔德声称可以用23种化学元素混合造雨。现在他正在配制为圣地亚哥造出38英寸大雨的原料。

圣地亚哥需要雨水，即使是好年景，也只有大约10英寸的雨水降落到这座加利福尼亚的城市。但是就是这个数字，在19世纪后期也在大大减少，严重的干旱正在威胁着这座城市。如果圣地亚哥想要扩大城市规模并且变得富有，水是必不可少的。

severe *adj.* 严重的

In 1897 the city came up with a plan. It built Morena Dam on a nearby river. The dam created a lake, or *reservoir*, to store rainwater. The dam seemed like a good solution. But it didn't work. There was never enough rain to fill up the reservoir.

By 1915 it was clear that something else had to be done. But what?

Enter Charles Hatfield, the rainmaker. He said he could make it rain. Only a few people believed him. Most thought he was a *fraud*. Still, he did seem to have a *knack* for bringing rain. At least, it seemed to rain when and where he said it would.

Eleven years earlier, Hatfield had been in Los Angeles, California, another dry city. Merchants there had promised Hatfield $50 if

---

这座城市在1897年曾经提出一项计划，即在附近的河流上建造莫雷纳水坝。水坝可以形成一个湖或者水库来储存雨水。建水坝看起来是一个不错的解决方案，但是并没有奏效，因为从来没有足够的雨水可以填满水库。

这种状况一直持续到了1915年，看来必须采取一些其他的措施了，但是又能怎么办呢？

造雨者查尔斯·海特菲尔德说他能让老天下雨。只有少数人相信他的话，大多数人认为他是个骗子。尽管如此，他看来确实有一套求雨的诀窍，至少他说什么时候或者在哪里下雨老天都会给面子。

早在11年前，海特菲尔德居住在加利福尼亚的另一座干旱城市洛杉矶的时候，那里的商人曾经许诺如果海特菲尔德能造出一英寸的雨水就给

---

reservoir *n.* 水库
knack *n.* 诀窍；本领

fraud *n.* 骗子

he could produce one inch of rain. Hatfield agreed. He told the merchants they would get their inch of rain within five days. And indeed, on the fourth day more than an inch of rain fell on Los Angeles. Hatfield walked away with $50.

Soon after that, a Los Angeles newspaper got in touch with Hatfield. It asked him to make 18 inches of rain fall in the first five months of 1905. If he did, the paper would pay him $1,000. Everyone thought it was a *gag*. They assumed it was just a way to sell papers. After all, it almost never rains that much in Los Angeles. Still, by the end of May, 18.22 inches of rain had fallen!

Hatfield claimed he brought the rain with a special "rain stew." First, he built a 20-foot-tall tower. Then he mixed up a batch of 23

他50美元。海特菲尔德同意了，并且告诉商人他们会在五天内得到那一英寸降雨。事实上，在第四天超过一英寸的雨水就降落到了洛杉矶，海特菲尔德揣着50美元走了。

那之后不久，一家洛杉矶的报纸联系到海特菲尔德并请求他在1905年的头五个月制造出18英寸的雨水，如果他成功了会得到1000美元的报酬。人们认为这只是一个噱头罢了，报社是想通过这个手段进行促销，毕竟在洛杉矶从来没有降过那么多的雨水。然而，到了五月底，洛杉矶的雨水足足降了18.22英寸。

海特菲尔德声称他是用一种特殊的化学混合物来降雨。首先他建造了一座20英尺高的塔楼，然后把23种不同的化学药品混为一炉。他从来不披

---

gag *n.* 噱头

different chemicals. He never revealed the *formula*. He did not even tell Paul, his brother and partner. Hatfield mixed all the chemicals together over a fire at the top of the tower and let the mixture *evaporate* into the air.

When people in San Diego heard about Hatfield, some wanted to hire him. A group called the Wide Awake Improvement Club thought it was worth a try. But the city council said no. Its members still hoped the dam was all they needed. The *debate* went on for years. So, too, did the dry weather.

Then in December 1915, Hatfield showed up at Morena Dam. He *boasted* that he could fill the reservoir. He said he could make it rain at least 40 inches within a year. The city would then have all

---

露配方，即使是对他的弟弟兼合作伙伴保罗也讳莫如深。海特菲尔德把所有的化学制品混合到一起放在塔楼顶端的火上，让混合物蒸发到大气之中。

当圣地亚哥的人听说到海特菲尔德的大名以后，一些人想要聘请他。一个叫作"全面唤醒进步俱乐部"的组织认为这值得一试。但是市政部门投了反对票，议员们依然抱有希望地认为水坝才是他们所需要的。关于是否聘请海特菲尔德的争论近数年，就像这干旱的天气一样持续着。

后来在1915年12月，海特菲尔德在莫雷纳水坝现身。他夸口称能把水库蓄满，说一年内至少可以降40英寸的雨量，这正是该城市所需要的用

---

formula *n.* 配方
debate *n.* 争论

evaporate *v.* 蒸发
boast *v.* 自夸

the water it needed. His fee for this feat, he said, was $10,000. By this time the city council was *desperate*. The members felt they had nothing to lose. So they agreed to hire him. The *council* members, however, did not sign the contract. But Hatfield did not notice. Or maybe he just thought their word was good enough.

In any case, on January 13, 1916, Hatfield and his brother Paul put up a 20-foot tower near Morena Dam. They laid a platform on the top and built a fire on it. Hatfield mixed his "rain stew" in a pot over the fire. Then he released the steam into the air and waited.

He did not have to wait long. The next morning clouds began to roll in. By noon it was raining hard. Still Hatfield kept his pot boiling. The Wide Awake Improvement Club was thrilled. So, too,

---

水量。他给自己的手艺开价10,000美金，此时的市政议员们实在已经黔驴技穷了，而且他们认为这笔钱并不算是损失，于是同意雇用海特菲尔德。然而，市政议员并没有签订合同，海特菲尔德也没有在意，或许他认为这些人的承诺已经足够了。

　　不管怎样，1916年1月13日海特菲尔德和他的弟弟在莫雷纳水坝旁搭起了一座20英尺高的塔楼。他们在塔顶铺设了一个平台，在上面燃起火堆。然后海特菲尔德把他的降雨用品混合到一起放到火上的锅里，让蒸气释放到空气之中，而后的事情就是等待了。

　　他没有等待太久的时间。第二天早晨乌云开始滚滚涌来，到了中午时分骤雨初至。此时海特菲尔德没有停止熬煮锅里的东西。全面唤醒进步俱

---

desperate *adj.* 绝望的　　　　　　　　　　　council *n.* 市政委员会

was everyone else. Suddenly the city's future looked bright. One newspaper headline *proclaimed*: "Downpour Lays Mantle of Wealth on San Diego."

For the next four days the rain came down in buckets. By the third day, people were starting to worry. They had never seen this much rain before. The whole month of January usually brought less than two inches of rain. Now close to 13 inches had fallen in just four days. Roads were under water. Floods washed out bridges. Homes floated away. Railroad tracks became *swamped*. People on one train had to be carried to dry land by boat! One man joked that the city should pay Hatfield $100,000 to stop the rain.

At last, on January 20, the rain stopped. The sun came out. It

---

乐部变得异常兴奋，现在人人都是如此，整个城市的前途突然变得一片光明。一家报纸的头版宣告："倾盆大雨为圣地亚哥铺上了一层财富。"

接下来的4天大雨丝毫没有收手的意思。到了第三天人们就已经开始担心，他们以前从来没有看过这么多的雨。通常整个一月的降雨量都不会超过2英寸，而现在仅仅4天之内已经接近了13英寸。马路被水淹没；洪流冲走了桥梁；房屋漂得没有了踪迹；铁轨也被浸泡，用船才能把火车上的乘客运送到没有被水淹的地方。一个人开玩笑说城市应该付给海特菲尔德10万美元让他把雨停了。

终于，在1月20日那天雨停了，太阳露出了笑脸。看起来仿佛厄运已

---

proclaim *v.* 声明；宣告　　　　　　　swamp *v.* 淹没；陷入困境

looked as if the worst was over. But it wasn't. Six days later the rain started again, harder than ever. The ground could not *absorb* any more water. The San Diego River overflowed its banks. More homes got washed away. All but two of the city's 112 bridges were swept away. At the Morena Dam the water level rose two feet an hour. Frightened engineers had to *divert* water away from the dam. Still the water level came within five inches of the top. Luckily, it didn't overflow. If it had, the resulting flood could have wiped out the whole city.

On January 29 the rain finally did end. By then 38 inches had fallen on San Diego. That was a record that still stands.

That day Charles and Paul Hatfield took down their tower. They

---

经结束了，但是6天之后大雨卷土重来，这一次更加猛烈。由于大地不再吸收更多的水分，圣地亚哥的河流开始溢出河岸。更多的房屋被大水冲垮；城中112座桥梁除了两座其余的都被卷走。莫雷纳大坝处的水位以每小时2英尺的速度上涨，胆战心惊的工程师们不得不转变水流的方向以保护大坝。可是水位线还是保持在距离坝顶5英尺的范围之内，幸运的是洪水没有溢出大坝，如果那样的话，整个城市将会遭受灭顶之灾。

1月29日，雨终于停了。此时的圣地亚哥已经降落了38英寸的雨水，迄今为止那还是一个记录。

那天查尔斯·海特菲尔德和保罗·海特菲尔德兄弟下了塔楼，他们把

---

absorb *v.* 吸收   divert *v.* 转向

swept up all clues as to the chemicals they had used. But as they worked, they heard that a *lynch mob* was headed their way. An angry *throng* of citizens vowed to kill Hatfield for flooding their city. The brothers slipped out of town before the mob could catch them.

Later, Hatfield tried to explain that the damage was not his fault. He said the city council was to blame. He had only done what they asked him to do. Maybe, he said, they shouldn't have wanted so much rain.

Hatfield tried to collect the $10,000 the city owed him. The council flatly refused to pay. The members pointed out that they had never signed the contract. They also pointed out the damage

曾经使用过的化学品清理得了无痕迹。正当他们清理的时候，兄弟俩听到了愤怒的人群乱哄哄地奔向他们而来。一大群怒气冲冲的居民发誓要杀了海特菲尔德，因为他淹没了整座城市。兄弟俩在人们捉到他们之前悄悄溜出了城去。

后来，海特菲尔德解释损失并不是他的过错，而应该怪罪市政委员会。他只不过按照他们吩咐的去做，他们或许就不应该要那么多的雨。

海特菲尔德尽全力去讨要圣地亚哥欠他的10,000美金，却遭到了市政委员会直截了当的拒绝。委员会成员们指出他们从来没有签过合同，同

lynch mob　施用私刑的暴民　　　　　　　　　　　　throng　*n.*　大群

that had been done to the city by the rain. Hatfield then lowered his demand to $4,000. That, he said, would just cover the cost of his chemicals. Still the council said no. In the end Hatfield got nothing from the city.

Did Charles Hatfield really cause the rain? Some people say he did. They think his *foul*-smelling "rain stew" did work. Years later, his brother Paul said, "After all, they are beginning to seed clouds [with chemicals] to make rain." Others disagree. They believe Hatfield was just lucky and a very good student of weather trends. They think he studied weather records and rain cycles and then guessed right about when it was going to rain. To this day no one knows the truth. So Hatfield the Rainmaker remains one of the mysteries of history.

时也指出大雨给城市带来的损失。而后海特菲尔德把价钱降低到4000美元，他说那只是一个成本价。市政部门依然拒绝支付，最后海特菲尔德一个子儿也没有从这个城市得到。

大雨真的是查尔斯·海特菲尔德制造出来的吗？有人说是他那气味难闻的降雨混合物起了作用。多年以后他的弟弟保罗说："毕竟，他们开始（用化学品）播云造雨。"其他人也有不同看法，他们相信海特菲尔德只是很幸运而且善于把握天气的趋势。他们认为他研究过天气的记录和雨水循环，而后正确推测出什么时候天会下雨。直至今日，没有人知道此事的真相。因此，这位造雨者海特菲尔德依旧是历史上的一个谜。

---

foul *adj.* 难闻的

7

What Happened to Amy?

Amy Bradley seemed to have it all. The 23-year-old Virginian was smart, *athletic*, and beautiful. She had been a star basketball player in college. Now, in early 1998, she had just moved into a new apartment. She was about to start a new job. *Best of all*, she

Because Amy Bradley has never been found, she remains on the FBI's Missing Persons list.

寻人启事
　　——离奇失踪的艾米

　　由于艾米·布拉德利一直没有被找到，她至今仍然在FBI的失踪人员名单中。

　　艾米·布拉德利看起来拥有一切。23岁的弗吉尼亚人聪明美丽而且身体健康，在大学时她就是一名篮球明星。1998年初，她刚刚搬进一所

---

athletic　*adj.* 体格健壮的　　　　　　　　　best of all　最重要的是

had been invited to go on a *cruise* with her parents and 21-year-old brother, Brad. But while on that cruise, something went wrong. Amy ended up missing. The story of how she *vanished* is both chilling and puzzling.

The first two days of the cruise went smoothly. Amy sent postcards to friends and picked up *souvenirs* to take home. She went swimming with her dad and shopping with her mom. She and Brad checked out the ship's casino. As she moved around the ship, Amy was careful not to get near the railing. She was afraid of heights. She was also afraid of ocean water. Amy didn't worry about drowning— in fact, she was a certified lifeguard. But she was squeamish about ocean creatures. She didn't like the idea of being in the water with sharks and jellyfish.

新的公寓，并且打算从事一份新的工作。最令她高兴的是，她已经接到邀请同父母以及21岁的弟弟布拉德一起去出海旅行。但是在船上的时候，发生了一些不可思议的事情，艾米失踪了。她失踪的经历听起来既让人毛骨悚然又有些疑惑不解。

海上旅行的头两天很顺利。艾米给她的几个朋友邮寄了明信片并且搜集了一些纪念品准备带回家。她和父亲游泳，和母亲购物还和弟弟去船上的娱乐场。当她在船上参观时，艾米很小心不靠近栏杆，她恐高而且害怕海水。艾米并不担心溺水——事实上她是一名持有证书的救生员。但是她很厌恶海洋生物，也不愿意有与鲨鱼和水母在水中共处的想法。

---

cruise *n.* 乘船游览   vanish *v.* 突然消失
souvenir *n.* 纪念品

Being attractive and outgoing, Amy received a lot of attention from the ship's passengers and crew. In those first two days she learned the names of several crew members. They all seemed friendly, and Amy had fun talking with them. One of these new *acquaintances* was a band member on the ship. Everyone called him "Yellow".

On the night of March 23, the third day of the trip, Brad and Amy went dancing in the ship's disco after enjoying a formal dinner with their parents. Yellow was there, and Amy talked with him for a while. She and Brad didn't return to their family's quarters until 3:45 the next morning. At that point Brad went to bed. Amy stretched out on a lounge chair on the balcony out-side the cabin. She was feeling a little seasick and wanted the fresh air.

因为长相迷人而且热情友好，船上的乘客和船员都很在意艾米。起初几天她就得知了几名船员的名字，他们看起来都很友好，艾米很愿意与他们交谈。这些新结识的人中有一位是船上的乐队成员，大家都称他"阿黄"。

3月23日的晚上，也就是旅行的第三天，与父母共进晚餐后布拉德与艾米去船上的迪斯科厅跳舞。阿黄也在那里，艾米与他说了一会话。她和布拉德直到第二天凌晨3:45才回到家人的住处。那时布拉德上床睡觉去了，艾米在舱室阳台上的一把躺椅中尽量伸着懒腰，她感到有点晕船，想要呼吸些新鲜空气。

---

acquaintance *n.* 认识的人；熟人

At about 5:30 A.M., Amy's father woke up and glanced out onto the *balcony*. He could not see Amy's face, but he did see her legs and feet on the lounge chair. Figuring she had fallen asleep out there, he saw no reason to rouse her. Instead, he just went back to sleep.

Half an hour later he thought he heard someone leaving the cabin. Waking up, he saw that Amy was gone. That surprised him because normally she was a late sleeper. Mr. Bradley knew she usually left notes telling the family where she had gone. So he looked around for one. But there was no note. *Perplexed*, he decided to go up to the main deck to look for her. For almost an hour, Mr. Bradley searched for Amy. He found no trace of her anywhere.

With panic rising in his chest, Mr. Bradley found one of the ship's

---

　　大约早晨5:30左右艾米的父亲醒来向舱外的阳台上扫了一眼。他看不到艾米的脸，但是他确实看到她的腿和脚还搭在躺椅上。父亲猜测她已在外面那儿睡着了就觉得没有必要唤醒她，他又回到了睡梦之中。

　　半个小时之后他感觉到有人离开舱室，醒来后发现艾米不见了。他感觉很意外，因为通常艾米睡得很沉，布拉德利先生知道她通常会给家人留下便条告知自己的去向，因此在舱里舱外到处寻找，但是没有找到任何留言。费解之中，他决定上主甲板去找她。布拉德利先生找了将近一个小时，但是在所有地方都没有发现艾米的踪迹。

　　布拉德利先生变得越发担心起来。他找到船上的一名官员，告诉那个

---

balcony *n.* 阳台　　　　　　　　　　perplexed *adj.* 困惑的；糊涂的

officers. He told the man Amy was missing. What happened next is in *dispute*. The Bradleys don't think the crew reacted with proper speed or concern. The cruise line, on the other hand, says the crew did everything they should have done. The ship's officers did not want to alarm the other guests. They thought Amy might be in someone's cabin or off in some little-used part of the ship.

By this time the ship had *docked* at the Caribbean island of Curacao. The Bradleys begged the officers to keep everyone on board until their daughter was found. But the officers didn't think that would be fair to the other passengers. So the gangplank was lowered, and many of the guests went ashore.

As the hours slipped by and there was still no sign of Amy, the Bradley family grew more and more *frantic*. Crew members, too,

---

人艾米失踪了，接下来是他们的一番争执。布拉德利一家觉得船上的工作人员没有对此事做出及时相应的反应。而另一方面，旅行团组织者说船员们已经尽了全力了。船上的官员不愿意惊扰其他的乘客，他们认为艾米可能在某人的舱室或者去了船上某个不常使用的部分。

这时候船已经驶入了加勒比的库拉索岛，布拉德利夫妇乞求官员们让人们待在船上直到找到他们的女儿。但是官员们认为那样对其他乘客不公平，因此跳板被放下，许多客人上了岸。

几个小时过去了，还是没有艾米的消息。布拉德利一家变得越来越惶

---

dispute *n.* 争执   dock *v.* （使船）进港
frantic *adj.* 紧张忙乱的

became more concerned. A search was made of the entire ship, but Amy wasn't found. Officials then began a search of the water. For three days planes and boats looked for Amy. The F.B.I, was called in. They found nothing.

What could have happened? At first the F.B.I wondered if Amy had killed herself by jumping overboard. But that didn't make sense. Everyone agreed she was a happy young woman with many plans for the future. She might have fallen *overboard* by accident. But that didn't seem likely, either. The railing came up to her chest. Besides, as her family said, it made her weak in the knees just to get near the ship's railing. Also, no body was found in the waters around Curacao.

恐不安，船上的工作人员也更加关注。他们进行了一次全船的彻底清查，但没有发现艾米，而后官员们开始到水中去搜寻。飞机和船只找了三天，还打电话请来了联邦调查局，然而他们也是一无所获。

到底发生了什么？起初联邦调查局想知道是不是艾米跳到海里自杀了。但是那讲不通，人人都知道她是一个快乐的年轻人，她给未来设计了十分美好的前途。会不会失足掉到船外呢？看来那也不太可能，船上的栏杆有齐胸高。此外按照她家人的说法，她一靠近栏杆就已经双腿发软站立不住了，而且在库拉索周围的水域中没有发现尸体。

---

overboard *adv.* 从船上落入/跳入水中

Had Amy run away? She could have put on a *disguise*. Then she could have walked off the ship with the other passengers in Curacao. The F.B.I considered this. But nothing about Amy fit the "runaway *profile*". She really had nothing to run away from. She got along very well with her family. She had plenty of friends and had recently adopted a dog. While on the trip, she had bought artwork for her new apartment and gifts for her friends.

That left the possibility of foul play. Could Amy have been kidnapped? Could a passenger or crew member have drugged her or cornered her somehow? Could the kidnapper have hidden her until he or she found a way to get her off the ship?

This idea terrified the Bradleys. But two clues seemed to point

---

难到艾米出走了吗？她可能穿上一身伪装在库拉索与其他乘客一起下了船，联邦调查局是这样认为的。但是没有什么原因能使得艾米符合上述的"出走特征"。她真的没有任何离家出走的理由。她与家人相处融洽，她有很多朋友，最近还养了一条狗。旅途中她还为新公寓购置了艺术品，为朋友选了礼物。

剩下的可能性只有暴力犯罪了，艾米会被人绑架吗？会不会某个乘客或者船员出于某种原因给她服了药物或者把她藏在某个角落呢？绑架者能不能把她藏起来直到自己设法带艾米离开这艘船呢？

这种想法使布拉德利一家愈发担心起来。两条线索正在把这个案子引

---

disguise *n.* 伪装物   profile *n.* 概述；简介

in that direction. First of all, two teenage girls on board the ship claimed to have seen Amy the morning she disappeared. They said she was with Yellow, the band member who had been so friendly. According to them, Amy and Yellow had been headed up to the disco room around 5:30 A.M.. About 15 minutes later Yellow had left that room alone.

The second clue came from a police *trainee* in Puerto Rico. He claimed he saw Amy on March 28. That was four days after she disappeared. It was also the day the ship stopped in Puerto Rico before heading back to the United States. The trainee said he saw a man forcing Amy into a taxi. He said she looked upset and *confused*. When the F.B.I questioned the trainee, he was indeed able to pick

---

到他们所担心的方向上来。其一，船上的两个十几岁的女孩称在艾米失踪的那天早晨看到过她，他们说她和阿黄在一起，就是那个很友善的乐队成员。据他们说艾米和阿黄在早晨5:30分向迪斯科厅走去，大约15分钟以后阿黄一个人离开了那间屋子。

第二条线索来自于波多黎各的一名警方实习生。他声称在3月28日看到过艾米，那是她失踪后的第四天，那天船在波多黎各靠岸停泊，然后准备掉头去美国。实习生说他看到一个男子强迫艾米上了出租车，他还看到艾米很慌乱不安。当联邦调查局询问实习生的时候，他的确能把艾米的照

---

trainee *n.* 实习生　　　　　　　　confused *adj.* 迷惑的；糊涂的

Amy's picture out of a line-up.

These clues pointed to trouble. But they also left many questions unanswered. For one thing, why had Amy left the family *cabin* so early on the morning of March 24? Where had she been going? Why didn't she leave a note?

Also, what motive would anyone have had for kidnapping her? Amy wasn't rich. She had no enemies. And if someone had nabbed her, where had she been hidden? Had she been somewhere on the ship as it sailed from Curacao to Puerto Rico? If so, why wasn't she found when the ship was searched? And why was no *ransom* note ever sent?

Finally, there was the question of Yellow. Had Amy really gone up

---

片从一堆人的中间挑出来。

　　这些线索表明了案子的棘手，但是也留有许多难以解答的问题。其一，为什么艾米在3月24日清晨要那么早离开家人的舱室呢？她要去哪里？她为什么不留下一张便条？

　　而且绑架她有什么动机呢？艾米不富有，也没有仇家。如果有人绑架了她，又能把她藏哪儿呢？当船从库拉索驶向波多黎各时，她在船上的某个地方吗？如果是这样搜船时为什么没有发现她呢？为什么至今没有收到索要赎金的便条呢？

　　最后，是阿黄的问题，3月24日艾米真的和他去了迪斯科厅吗？船上

---

cabin　n.　（轮船上工作或生活的）隔间　　　　ransom　n.　赎金

to the disco room with him on the morning of March 24? If so, why? Was he somehow involved in her *disappearance*? Cruise officials said he passed a lie *detector* test. But why would the teenage witnesses lie?

The Bradley family did everything they could to find Amy. They hired private detectives. They made trips back to the Caribbean themselves. They even offered a $260,000 reward for Amy's safe return. Nothing worked.

As time passed, many people feared Amy was dead. The Bradleys refused to give up hope. But officials had run out of ideas. So Amy Bradley remains on the missing persons' list. And Amy's family is left with many haunting questions, but no good answers.

的官员说他通过了测谎仪的测试。但是那两个女孩目击者说谎的目的是什么呢？

布拉德利一家尽自己的最大努力去寻找艾米。他们雇用的私家侦探亲自坐船返回了加勒比，甚至为了艾米的安全返回悬赏26万美元的奖金，但是这一切都没有得到任何结果。

随着时间的推移，很多人担心艾米已经死了。布拉德利一家拒绝放弃，但是官方已经束手无策了。因此在失踪人员的名单上，还有着艾米·布拉德利的名字。她的家人仍然有许多疑问萦绕在心头，但是至今也没有一个明确的答案。

---

disappearance *n.* 消失　　　　　　　　　　　detector *n.* 探测器

Mysterious Circles

O ne morning in 1976 a farm worker in Hampshire, England, saw a strange sight. There was an *odd* circle in a field near highway A34. When the man checked it out, he grew even more puzzled. A perfectly round section of the field had been *flattened*. The

These complex crop circles were found in a wheat field in England.

麦田怪圈
——田地里的神秘图案

这些农作物构成的复杂的圆圈出现在英格兰的麦田里。

1976年的一天早晨，英格兰汉普郡的一位农场工人发现了奇怪的景象，在A34号高速公路旁的农田里出现了一个古怪的圆圈。这名工人仔细地检查了一遍后，他变得更加摸不着头脑——田地被整齐地压倒了一片，谷物的茎梗呈螺旋式弯曲，四周没有脚印，也没有任何人走过、跑过或者

---

odd *adj.* 奇怪的　　　　　　　　　　flatten *v.* 变平；使……平坦

stalks of grain were bent over in a *swirling* pattern. There were no footprints around. There was no sign that anyone had walked, run, or driven through the field.

Word of this mysterious "crop circle" spread quickly. Soon people spotted similar circles in other fields. The circles were most often found where some kind of grain was growing. But once in a while they appeared in other places. For instance, they were found among sugar *beets*. They were also found among soybeans and potato plants. Most of the circles were quite large. They might be 50 or 100 feet in diameter. A few were even bigger than football fields.

Most of the circles appeared in southern England. But some were found as far away as New Zealand and Japan. There was really no telling when or where the next crop circle was going to pop up. The circles always appeared within the space of a few hours. At *twilight* a

---

驱车驶过田地的痕迹。

有关这神秘的"麦田圈"的消息很快传播开了。很快人们在其他的地里也发现了相似的圆圈。这种圆圈最常出现在某种谷物生长的地方，但偶尔也出现在别的地方，比如在甜菜地中。有人也曾经在大豆和西红柿地中发现过怪圈。这种圆圈大多都很大，直径可以达到50或100英尺，有几个甚至比足球场还大。

大多数圆圈出现在南英格兰，但是有些也出现在像新西兰和日本那么远的地方。没有人能推断出下一次怪圈会在什么时候出现，出现在哪里。圆圈总是在几个小时的范围内就迅速出现。黄昏时候田地里看起来一切正

---

stalk *n.* （叶）柄；（花）梗
beet *n.* 甜菜

swirl *v.* 打旋；旋动
twilight *n.* 黄昏

field would look perfectly ordinary. By the next morning, there would be a big circle stamped on it. Once in a while, neighbors reported hearing a humming noise in the night. A few claimed they saw a bright light. But most of the time they noticed nothing at all.

Sometimes the crop circle was just that—a circle. On occasion, though, it was more complex. The design might feature a small circle inside a larger ring. There might be several circles side by side. Once in a while the circles had long lines that looked like tails. A few of the circles were found inside *rectangles* or other shapes.

At first skeptics thought the crop circles were a joke. They figured somebody was going out into fields and stomping on crops. But it wasn't that simple. To be sure, a few *pranksters* did make their own circles. But these fake ones were easy to spot. Footprints could be seen around the edges of the fake circles. The crop would be

---

常，但是第二天早晨，上面就会被踏出个大圆圈。曾经有邻居说晚上听到了嗡嗡的噪音，有几个人还声称他们看见了一道亮光，但是大多数时候他们根本什么都没有注意到。

有时候"麦田圈"就是那么一个圆圈。然而有时它更复杂，图案可能是小圈套在大圈里；一起共有数个圆圈并排在一起；有时候这些圈带有长线就像尾巴一样；有几个圈内有矩形或者其他的图案。

起初持怀疑态度者认为"麦田圈"只不过是个笑话，他们猜测那是有人到田地里踩踏庄稼形成的。但事实并不是那么简单。为了确定这种观点的正确，几个恶作剧者确实制造了这样的圆圈。但是这些假圆圈很容易被识破，因为假圆圈的边缘四周能看到脚印，靴子走过的地方庄稼被踩踏得

---

rectangle n. 矩形；长方形   prankster n. 恶作剧的人

trampled and pushed into the ground wherever someone's boots had stepped.

With real crop circles, though, there were not any footprints. This was true even in muddy fields where it was impossible to walk without leaving tracks. One circle was seen on a snow-covered mountain in Afghanistan. There were no crops there. But the snow was packed down in the same swirling pattern. And not a single footprint led to or from the site.

When researchers began studying the circles, they discovered another interesting fact. There was *evidence* that crop circles had actually been around since well before 1976. Several books from the Middle Ages mention them. Many ancient stone carvings look similar to the shapes in the fields. If they are a joke, it's one that has been around for a long time.

贴伏到地面上。

然而真正的"麦田圈"周围没有任何脚印，即使在只要走过就一定会留下痕迹的泥泞田地也是如此。有人曾经在阿富汗白雪覆盖的山上见到一个圆圈。那里没有庄稼，但是雪以同样的漩涡状被压下去，当场没有一个脚印走来或者走去。

当研究员开始研究这些圆圈时，他们发现了另一个有趣的事实。有证据表明有关"麦田圈"的报道在1976年以前实际上就已广为流传。几部中世纪的书籍中曾经提及过许多古代石雕看起来就像田地中的那些圈的形状。如果那些圆圈是笑话，那也是流传了很长时间的笑话。

---

trample *v.* 踩碎；践踏　　　　　　　　　evidence *n.* 证据

A Scottish professor studying the circles explained why he didn't think they were *hoaxes*. "The crops around them are not disturbed at all," he said, "and the patterns are formed too perfectly."

Some people thought animals were making the circles. They thought *hedgehogs* could be the *culprits*. Hedgehogs do run in wild circles when they are mating. But that would not explain the absence of tracks. And it wouldn't explain how circles were made in rice paddies and other places where no hedgehogs live.

A few people thought helicopters might be to blame. If a helicopter hovered over a field, the wind from its *rotors* might flatten the crops. But that theory did not work, either. The circles often appeared in places where no helicopters had been flying.

The more scientists studied the crop circles, the deeper the mystery got. They found that the circles did not kill the crops. In fake

---

一位研究过这些圆圈的苏格兰教授解释说他认为那不是个骗局。因为"圆圈周围的庄稼根本没有受到任何损伤，"他说，"而且图案构成的也相当完美"。

有人认为这些圆圈的制造者是动物，他们认为罪魁祸首可能是刺猬。刺猬在交配时会在野外疯狂地跑圈，但那无法解释没有足迹的原因，也解释不了在稻田或者其他没有刺猬居住的地方怪圈是如何形成的。

也有人认为应该归咎于直升机——如果直升机在田地上空盘旋，螺旋桨发出的风会压平庄稼。但是这个理论不能成立，圆圈经常出现在没有直升机飞过的地方。

科学家对"麦田圈"研究的越多，它就变得越发神秘。他们发现圆圈

---

hoax *n.* 骗局；恶作剧
culprit *n.* 罪犯

hedgehog *n.* 刺猬
rotor *n.* 转动部件

circles, the plants were trampled and broken. But in real ones, the plants were simply bent. It is quite easy to bend young plants. But as plants get older they become less *flexible*. It was hard to imagine how anyone could have bent fully-grown crops without destroying them.

One scientist spent years looking at crop circles. He found some made from stalks an inch thick. These stalks would snap if he tried to bend them more than 20 or 30 degrees. Yet in the crop circles these stalks were bent right over to the ground. He said, "I found many stems bent 120 degrees without the slightest snapping or splitting."

In the 1980s, another scientist came up with a new theory. He thought the circles might be formed by *whirlwinds*, or "spinning balls of air." He believed these balls became charged with electricity.

没有伤害到庄稼。在人为制造的圆圈中，植物被踩倒并且折断；但是在真正的怪圈中植物只是弯曲。把植物的幼苗弄弯曲是比较容易的，但是当植物长成以后再弯曲它们就不那么简单了，因为它们的柔韧性变得很小。很难想象有谁能把完全长成的植物弄弯曲却不损伤到他们。

一位科学家花费了几年时间观察"麦田圈"。他发现有些圆圈是一英寸粗的庄稼压倒后形成的。如果他试着折那些植物的茎超过20或30度，它们会啪的一声折断；而在"麦田圈"中这些茎直接弯到了地面上。"我发现许多茎弯了120度却没有任何哪怕最微小的断裂或者破损。"

20世纪80年代，另一名科学家提出了一个新的理论。他认为圆圈有可能是由旋风或者"气旋"形成。他相信这些气团带电，在接触地面时他

---

flexible *adj.* 灵活的；可弯曲的　　　　　　　　whirlwind *n.* 旋风

When they touched the ground, they somehow shocked the plants. That caused the plants to bend.

Then another *bizarre* fact emerged. A scientist studying the cells of crop circle plants found that the cells were not normal. They were long and stretched out. When plants were grown from these seeds, the results were funny-shaped plants that grew bigger and quicker than they should have. The researcher agreed with the theory that whirlwinds created the circles, but believed the whirlwinds were full of microwave energy. These *microwaves* could heat the plants. That could make them soft enough to bend. The microwaves could also change the shape of the plants' cells.

Still, no one could say where the whirlwinds were coming from

---

们以某种方式电击了植物，从而引起植物弯曲。

接下来另外一件不可思议的事情出现了。一名研究庄稼圈细胞的科学家发现那些细胞很不正常。这些细胞很长而且向外伸展，它们的种子长出的植物形状古怪且比原来更大更快。研究人员同意旋风产生圆圈的理论，但是他们认为旋风充满了微波能量，这些微波能加热植物，使得植物变软从而弯曲。微波也能改变植物细胞的形状。

然而，没有人知道旋风来自哪里，又是如何形成的。某些人认为旋风的说法不值一提，这些人开始寻找不同的答案。他们想知道"麦田圈"是

---

bizarre *adj.* 异乎寻常的   microwave *n.* 微波

or how they were made. And to some people, the idea of whirlwinds did not make sense anyway. These people began to look for different answers. They wondered if crop circles were the work of aliens. They thought UFOs might be making the circles.

Many researchers did not believe this theory, but without another explanation, it was hard to rule it out. "This could be beyond science," admitted one scientist, who claimed to be skeptical about UFOs. "A very high level of *intelligence* is in control here."

To this day, no one knows what causes crop circles. But they keep coming. Every summer hundreds of them appear without warning. So who knows? Maybe it's just one of those mysteries that keeps going around and around.

否是外星人的杰作。他们认为可能是不明飞行物制造了这些圆圈。

许多研究者不相信这个理论，但是没有其他更合理的解释，所以难以把它排除掉。"这不符合科学，"一位科学家承认，他声称对不明飞行物表示怀疑。"一种更高智力的生物正在控制这里。"

迄今为止，没有人知道"麦田圈"是如何形成的。但是它们不断地造访，每年夏天数百个"麦田圈"毫无征兆地现身。所以谁会知道答案呢？也许那只是一个继续流传下去的谜吧！

---

intelligence *n.* 智力

9

Cuban Stowaway

Twenty-two-year-old Armando Socarras wanted to leave Cuba. So did his 16-year-old friend Jorge Perez. They opposed Cuba's government and thought they could find more freedom and *opportunity* in Europe or the United States. Other

Armando Socarras survived nine hours in a wheel well on a flight from Cuba to Madrid, Spain.

古巴偷渡者

阿曼多·索克拉斯在起落架舱中呆了9个小时而幸存了下来。那架飞机是从古巴飞往西班牙的马德里的。

22岁的阿曼多·索克拉斯想要离开古巴，他16岁的朋友乔治·佩雷斯也是。他们反对古巴政府，认为在欧洲或者美国他们可以找到更多的自由和机

opportunity *n.* 机会

Cubans felt the same way. Many had already fled their island nation in the Caribbean Sea. Most did it by boat. Socarras and Perez tried a different approach.

On June 4, 1969, the two young men went to the airport in Havana, Cuba. They hid in the tall grass near the runway. A passenger jet was about to take off for a nine-hour flight to Madrid, Spain. Socarras and Perez didn't have tickets for the flight. Instead, they planned to be *stowaways*.

Socarras and Perez knew they couldn't sneak into the plane. So they planned to hide on the outside of the plane. Every jet has two big wheel wells. These are spaces on the underside of the plane's body. During flight, the wheels are *tucked* up into these wells. Socarras and Perez thought they could squeeze

---

会。其他的古巴人也这样认为，许多古巴人逃离了古巴来到加勒比海。大部分人是通过船只到达目的地，索克拉斯和佩雷斯尝试了不同的方法。

1969年6月4日，两个年轻人来到了古巴的哈瓦那国际机场，他们躲藏在跑道附近高高的草丛里面。一架客机即将开始飞往西班牙马德里的9小时航程。索克拉斯和佩雷斯没有这个航班的机票，实际上他们准备偷渡。

索克拉斯和佩雷斯知道无法溜进机舱，所以他们计划躲在飞机的外面。每架喷气式飞机都有两个巨大的起落架舱，位于飞机机身的下部。在飞行中，它们会折起进入这些起落架舱里面。索克拉斯和佩雷斯认为他们

---

stowaway *n.* 偷渡者   tuck *v.* 折叠；收拢

into one of the wheel wells and ride there all the way to Spain.

When no one was looking, they ran out onto the runway and climbed into the right wheel well. Then they hung on for dear life as the *jet* took off.

Once the plane was in the air the pilot pushed a lever. That lifted the wheels up into their wells. But something was wrong. The pilot saw his control light flickering. That meant the wheels were not fully closed within the wells. The *pilot* thought something might be stuck, so he lowered the wheels again. When he raised them a second time, the control light went out. The wheels were now fully closed within the well, and the pilot thought nothing more about it.

Back in the wheel well, Socarras and Perez found the wheels pressed up against them. They had little space to move. But that

---

可以蜷缩在其中一个舱室中，一直飞到西班牙。

当没有人看的时候，他们冲上跑道，钻进了右面起落架室。然后在飞机起飞时，他们就命垂一线了。

飞机升空后，飞行员推下了一个杠杆，这使起落架升到机舱里面。但是出现了问题，飞行员看到它的控制灯在闪烁，那意味着起落架没有完全折叠好。飞行员认为里面可能有什么东西塞住了，所以他再次放下了起落架。当他第二次抬起起落架时，故障信号消失了。这次起落架在舱室里面完全折叠好了，飞行员没有再继续考虑这个问题。

回到起落架舱里面，索克拉斯和佩雷斯发现起落架紧紧地压住了他

---

jet *n.* 喷气式飞机；喷射引擎　　　　　　　　　　　　pilot *n.* 飞行员

was the least of their problems. Both of them were lightly dressed. Socarras wore just a cotton shirt and pants. As the jet climbed, the air grew much colder. By the time the plane reached 30,000 feet the temperature had dropped to 40 degrees below zero! "Little by little I felt cold, sleepy, and had great pains in my ears," Socarras later said. "I must have fallen asleep. I don't know anything more. I know that I woke up once thinking it was terribly cold."

Amazingly, though, Socarras made it. When the plane came to a stop, he fell out of the wheel well. He was *unconscious*. His clothes were coated with ice. Somewhere along the way he had lost a shoe. His hands, arms, and legs were *frostbitten*. But he was alive. Jorge Perez was not so lucky. Socarras said that he rode with him throughout the flight, but Perez was not in the wheel well when the

---

们。他们几乎没有空间可移动，但那是他们遇到的最小的问题。两个人穿得很少。索克拉斯仅仅穿了一个棉布衫和裤子。随着飞机的升高，空气变得寒冷。当飞机升到30,000英尺的高空时，气温下降到了零下40摄氏度！"渐渐地，我感到寒冷、困倦，耳朵中出现剧烈的疼痛，"后来索克拉斯回忆到，"我一定是睡着了，什么也不知道了，我记得我醒来一次，感到极度的寒冷。"

但是令人惊奇的是，索克拉斯成功了。当飞机停下来时，他从起落架舱中掉了出来。他已经失去了知觉，衣服上面布满了冰。在飞行中，不知什么地方他丢掉了一只鞋。他的手、胳膊和腿都有冻伤，但是他还活着。但是乔治·佩雷斯却没有那么幸运。索克拉斯说在整个航程中他都和他在

---

unconscious *adj.* 无意识的   frostbitten *adj.* 被冻伤的

plane landed in Madrid. It is believed that he fell out when the pilot lowered the wheels to land.

When airport workers found Socarras, they rushed him to the hospital. Doctors soaked his frostbitten limbs in warm water. A short time later, Socarras regained consciousness. Except for signs of exposure and shock, he was in fairly good shape.

No one could believe it. The chief engineer for the company that had built the jet called Socarras's survival "a *miracle*." He pointed out that there was very little room in the wheel well. He said there was "one chance in a million" that the wheels wouldn't crush someone to death when they were pulled in.

Doctors, meanwhile, were stunned by the medical aspects of the case. They wondered how Socarras had survived without an *oxygen*

一起，但是当飞机在马德里机场降落时，佩雷斯却没有在舱室中。可能是驾驶员在打开起落架准备降落时他掉了下去。

当机场的工作人员发现索克拉斯时，他们急忙把他送到了医院。医生们把他冻伤的四肢放到温水中。一会儿，索克拉斯重新恢复了知觉。除了阳光灼伤和休克的症状外，他的健康状况还算不错。

没有人可以相信。飞机制造公司的总工程师称他的幸存是"一个奇迹"。他说起落架舱中的空间很小，如果有人被拖入了舱室，只有百万分之一的机会不会被起落架挤压致死。

医生们同时因为这个事件的医学方面而震惊。他们很奇怪没有氧气

---

miracle *n.* 奇迹   oxygen *n.* 氧气

mask. There is oxygen at 30,000 feet. But there isn't much. There is only about one-fourth the amount found at sea level. Mountain climbers use bottled oxygen when they go above 25,000 feet. A few climbers go higher without it. But they spend weeks getting their bodies used to the thin air.

Then there was the lack of air pressure. The 143 people inside the jet rode in comfort because the cabin was pressurized. But Socarras was out in the open. Air pressure at 30,000 feet is only one-third of what it is at sea level. A rapid drop in air pressure causes gas *bubbles* to form in the blood. The result is a bad case of the "bends." Getting the bends can lead to *paralysis* and even death. No one could understand how Socarras had avoided this fate.

罩，索克拉斯怎么能活下来。在30,000英尺的高度有氧气，但是并不多，那里只有海平面氧气量的四分之一。登山运动员攀登25,000英尺以上的高度时，使用瓶装的氧气。一些登山运动员不使用氧气攀登到高处，但是他们需要用几个星期的时间来适应稀薄的空气。

　　然后还有缺乏气压。机舱中的143名乘客可以很舒适，因为机舱是密封的。但是索克拉斯处于完全没有防护的外面。30,000英尺高度的气压只有海平面气压的三分之一，气压的迅速下降会导致血液中出现气泡，其结果是严重的"减压病"。减压病能够导致瘫痪甚至死亡。没有人知道索克拉斯是怎么样逃过了这个劫数的。

---

bubble *n.* 气泡；泡　　　　　　　　　　　　paralysis *n.* 瘫痪

Finally there was the cold air. Socarras had spent hours in air that was 40 degrees below zero. And he had done it dressed just in light cotton clothes. When he got to Spain, his body temperature had dropped to 93 degrees. That's almost six degrees below normal.

Without doubt, the *combination* of little oxygen, low air *pressure*, and severe cold should have killed him. The human body is not built to survive such great extremes. The doctors could not explain it. Said one, "Very few human hearts, if any, have endured what [Socarras's] heart did."

In the end, some doctors thought Socarras might have survived the lack of oxygen because of the extreme cold. When a human body cools down, it needs less and less oxygen. Everything starts

---

最后还有冷空气。索克拉斯在零下40摄氏度的低温环境下待了几个小时。而且他只是穿了单薄的棉布衣服。当他到达西班牙时，他的体温已经下降到了93度，这几乎比正常温度低6度。

毫无疑问，缺氧、低气压和严寒本来应该要了他的命。人体的构造是无法抵御这样的极端环境的。医生们也无法解释。一名医生说："如果有的话，也是极少数人的心脏能够承受 [索克拉斯的] 心脏承受过的经历。"

最后，一些医生认为，索克拉斯可能是因为严寒才在缺氧的状态下幸存了下来。当人体的温度降低时，它对氧气的需求越来越少，所有的功

---

combination *n.* 结合；组合；混合　　　　　　　pressure *n.* 气压；压力

shutting down. The heart pumps more slowly. The lungs take in less air. If the cooling happens at just the right speed, a person might live. One doctor said that if Socarras had been *chilled* too fast, it would have been *fatal*. But if his body cooled gradually, its demand for oxygen could have kept up with the supply. In other words, he wouldn't need much oxygen because he was almost frozen.

Everyone agreed that Socarras was very lucky to be alive. Since 1969, many other people have fled Cuba. But it is no surprise that none have copied Socarras's means of escape. As one doctor said, "[riding in the wheel well of a jet] is not likely to become a popular way to travel."

能开始关闭。心脏跳动更加缓慢，肺吸入更少的空气。如果这个降温的速度正确，人可以存活下来。一名医生说，如果索克拉斯降温太快，结果可能是致命的。但是如果他的身体是逐步降温，氧气的需求就能够和供应持平。换句话说，因为他几乎被冻僵了，所以他不可能需要太多的氧气。

所有人都认为索克拉斯能够活下来真是太幸运了。从1969年开始，许多人离开了古巴，但是没有人以索克拉斯的方式逃脱。正如一名医生所说的："[乘坐在起落架舱里面] 不可能成为一种流行的旅行方式。"

---

chill *v.* 使变冷　　　　　　　　　　　　fatal *adj.* 致命的

10

A Living Fossil

What would you say if someone claimed to have found a live *dinosaur*? You'd probably say he or she was crazy. Everyone knows the dinosaurs died out tens of millions of years ago. The only place you can find one these days is in a museum.

The coelacanth has been on the earth for more than 80 million years. Scientists had thought coelacanths were extinct until a live one was found off the coast of South Africa in 1938.

活化石

腔棘鱼，它已经在地球上存在八千万年了。科学家本来认为腔棘鱼已经灭绝了，但是1938年，在南非海岸找到了一条活鱼。

如果有人说找到了一条活的恐龙你会怎么说？你可能会说他/她是疯子。每个人都知道恐龙在几千万年前就已经灭绝了。现在你能够找到它们，唯一的地方就是博物馆。

dinosaur *n.* 恐龙

So was Marjorie Courtney-Latimer crazy? In 1938, she was working at a museum in South Africa. Her job was to collect fish *specimens*. One day she got a call from a fisherman who had been helping her find different kinds of fish. He had just brought in a fresh load of fish and wanted to show it to her. He thought it might contain some new specimens.

When Courtney-Latimer got to the dock, she spotted one very strange fish. It didn't look like anything she had seen before. It was blue and about five feet long. "[It was] the most beautiful fish I had ever seen," she wrote. But she had no idea what it was. Unfortunately, it was already dead. Still, she decided it was worth keeping. She wrapped it in rags soaked with *formaldehyde*. That

---

那么马加里·考特尼·拉提莫疯了吗？1938年，她在南非的一家博物馆工作。她的工作是收集鱼类的标本。一天，一名一直帮助她收集各种鱼类标本的渔民来找她。他刚刚捕了一大舱鱼，想要展示给她，说里面可能有新的标本种类。

当考特尼·拉提莫抵达码头时，她发现了一种十分奇怪的鱼。这种鱼她以前根本没有见过。它是蓝色的，大约5英尺长。"[这是]我见到的最漂亮的鱼，"她写道。但是她不知道它是什么东西。不幸的是它已经死了。但是她觉得这条鱼值得保存。她用浸有甲醛的布把它裹好，但是却没

---

specimen *n.* 标本　　　　　　　　　　　　　　formaldehyde *n.* 甲醛

didn't work well. The flesh quickly rotted away. All that remained was the skin and a few bones.

Back at the museum, Courtney-Latimer looked through her books to see if she could find out what the fish was. She could not believe what she learned. The strange fish looked just like a *coelacanth*. But that was impossible! The coelacanth had been *extinct* for 80 million years. It was wiped out long before the dinosaurs. Humans knew about it only because of *fossils* that had been found.

Still, Courtney-Latimer thought her fish could be a coelacanth. She told her boss about it. He said she must be mistaken. He said the fish was probably just a rock *cod*.

Courtney-Latimer refused to let the matter drop. She sent a detailed sketch to Professor J. L. B. Smith, an expert on fish. Smith

---

有效果，肉很快就烂掉了，剩下的只有皮肤和一些骨头。

回到了博物馆，考特尼·拉提莫查看了她的书，看看里面能否查出来这到底是什么鱼。她无法相信她所找到的结果。这条奇怪的鱼看起来就好像是腔棘鱼。但是不可能啊！腔棘鱼八千万年前就已经灭绝了，早在恐龙前就已经灭绝了。人们知道这种鱼仅仅因为人们发现过这种鱼的化石。

但是，考特尼·拉提莫认为她的鱼是腔棘鱼。她向她的老板报告了这个情况，他说她一定是弄错了，那条鱼也许是一条石斑鳕鱼。

考特尼·拉提莫不想就这样放下这个事情。她画了一个很详细的素描寄给了J.L.B.史密斯教授，他是一位研究鱼类的专家。史密斯震惊了。这

---

coelacanth *n.* 腔棘鱼
fossil *n.* 化石

extinct *adj.* 灭绝的
cod *n.* 鳕鱼

was stunned. The sketch looked like a coelacanth to him. He came to see the remains for himself. That convinced him. He believed Courtney-Latimer really had found a fish that dated back 80 million years.

Smith wanted to get his hands on a second coelacanth. Then he could document the discovery. He could prove beyond any doubt that the prehistoric fish was still alive. He sent notices to fishing villages in many parts of the world. The notice described the coelacanth. This fish can be four or five feet long. It does not have regular flat fins. Instead, it has *stumpy* rounded *lobes*. These lobes are jointed. They are almost like arms and legs. The coelacanth also has a bony head, small sharp teeth, and heavy scales.

In the notice Smith offered a reward of 100 pounds. The money

---

个素描在他看来就是腔棘鱼。他亲自来看鱼的残骸，这更使他相信。他相信考特尼·拉提莫的确是发现了八千万年前的鱼类。

史密斯想要亲自获得一条腔棘鱼，那样他就会记录这个发现，毫无疑问地证明这种史前的鱼类还生存着。他给世界上的许多渔村发去了通知。通知描绘了腔棘鱼的样子，这种鱼可能有4或5英尺长。它没有通常的平鳍，而是一种短粗的圆形叶。这些叶是相连着的，它们就好像是胳膊和腿一样。腔棘鱼也有一个骨质的头，小的尖利牙齿和大的鳞片。

通知上，史密斯提供了100英镑的奖金。这笔奖金将送给任何捕到第二条腔棘鱼的人。很长时间过去了，没有人做到。1952年，一名渔民在

---

stumpy *adj.* 短而粗的   lobe *n.* （身体器官的）叶

would be paid to anyone who caught a second coelacanth. For a very long time no one did. Then, in 1952, a fisherman pulled up an odd-looking fish off the coast of the Comoro Islands. He showed it to a friend who remembered Smith's notice.

Smith rushed to see the fish. It was indeed a coelacanth. Smith was so moved by the sight that he began to weep. This was the *zoological* find of the century. But it also raised questions. How could a fish that had been "dead" for so long reappear? All the coelacanth fossils were 80 million years old. If the species was still swimming around, why hadn't more recent remains been found?

Scientists think they have figured out the answer. Perhaps 80 million years ago the fish lived in *regions* where fossils could be left. Later, the fish moved to regions that didn't produce fossils. So it didn't leave a record that could be traced.

科摩罗群岛附近拉上来一条看起来很奇怪的鱼。他把它拿给一个朋友看，那个朋友还记得史密斯的通知。

史密斯马上前去看这条鱼，这的确是一条腔棘鱼。史密斯被这个场面深深地感动了，他开始哭泣。这是整个世纪以来动物学上的大发现，但是它也提出了问题。一种"死去"这么久的鱼怎么会再次出现呢？所有的腔棘鱼化石都是八千万年前的。如果这个物种还在到处游着，那么更近期的残骸怎么没有找到？

科学家们认为他们已经得出了答案。可能在八千万年前，这种鱼生活在能够留下化石的地方。后来这种鱼移居到了不能生产化石的地方，所以没有留下可以跟踪的记录。

---

zoological *adj.* 动物学的   region *n.* 地区；区域

In addition, the fish lives deep down in the ocean. The one Smith saw had come from 600 feet below the surface. The species can live as far down as 2,000 feet. Most fishermen did not look for fish in such deep waters. Once in a great while a local fisherman would come *ashore* with one. But they never realized what they had in their nets. They wanted to catch fish that could be sold for food. Since this fish had no useful flesh, it was seen as little more than a *nuisance*.

Since 1952, more than two hundred coelacanths have been caught. Sadly, none have lived more than a day. These fish can't survive in shallow water. They are used to living at the immense pressure found deep in the ocean. The lighter pressure at sea level kills them, often within just a few hours. Also, surface waters are

---

而且这种鱼生活在海洋的深处。史密斯见到的那一条是从海面下600英尺深的地方打捞上来的。这个物种甚至可以在2000英尺的深处生存，大部分渔民是不在这样的深处搜索鱼的。相隔很长时间，渔民可能会碰到一条。但是他们压根就没有意识到他们的网中有什么，他们希望能够卖掉它们作为食品。因为这种鱼没有有用的肉，所以它不过是个讨厌的东西。

从1952年开始，有200多条腔棘鱼被打捞了上来。可悲的是没有任何一条能够活过一天，这种鱼不能在浅水中生存。它们习惯于深海中强大的压力，海面上很轻的压力杀死了它们，经常就是几个小时的时间，而且表

---

ashore *adv.* 向（或在）岸上　　　　　　　　nuisance *n.* 讨厌的人（或事物）

much too warm for them.

The amazing story of this fish has one more chapter. Until recently, experts thought coelacanths lived in just one place. That was off the coast of the Comoro Islands. A few had been caught as far away as South Africa. But those were thought to be *strays*.

In 1998, however, marine biologist Mark Erdmann was in Indonesia with his wife. While shopping one day, his wife saw a strange *creature* in a wooden cart. It did not look like any fish she had ever seen. She told Erdmann about it. He took one look and knew right away it was a coelacanth. But how could that be? These fish had never been seen east of Madagascar. Now here was one 6,000 miles away!

Erdmann later found out that fisherman in those parts caught

面的水温对于它们来说也太温暖了。

关于这种鱼的故事可以是下一章。直到最近,专家们认为腔棘鱼仅仅生活在一个地方,那就是在科摩多群岛的附近。在很远的南非海岸也捕捞到过一些,但是那些鱼被认为是离群索居的。

但是,在1998年,海洋生物学家马克·厄得曼和他的妻子来到了印度尼西亚。一天在购物时,他的妻子在一辆木头大车上看到了一个奇怪的生物。它与她以前见过的任何鱼类都不同。她和厄得曼讲述了这个东西。他看了一眼马上就知道了是腔棘鱼。但这是怎么回事呢?这种鱼在马达加斯加东部从来就没有出现过,这里距离那里有6000英里!

厄得曼后来得知,那里的渔民每年会捕捞上来2至3条。一天他甚至

---

stray *n.* 离群的动物   creature *n.* 生物

two or three coelacanths a year. One day, he even saw one hauled ashore in a shark net. It was still alive. The fish lived for six hours. That gave Erdmann time to photograph and study it. It looked just like the ones found off the coast of Africa. The only difference was the color. The African ones were *pale* blue with white marks. This one was a mix of brown and gray.

Are there more surprises in store? No one knows. But scientists think there are only about 500 of these creatures left in the world. That's a very small number. It's so small, in fact, that the fish has been put on the endangered species list. As fishermen cast nets deeper and deeper into the ocean, they keep bringing up coelacanths. "[The fish] could disappear in the next 15 to 20 years," says one marine *biologist*.

在一条拖上来的捕鲨网中发现了一条，它还活着，那条鱼活了6个小时。这给厄得曼以充足的时间来拍照并且研究它。它看起来与非洲沿岸的一样，唯一的不同就是颜色。非洲的是浅蓝色上面带有白色的斑点，而这一条是棕色和灰色的混合。

是不是还有我们没有发现的奇异的事？没有人知道。但是科学家们认为世界上大约只幸存500条这样的鱼。这是一个很小的数额，数额太小了以至于人们甚至把它列入了濒危物种。随着渔民的渔网越来越深，他们不断地捞上来腔棘鱼。"在以后的15至20年，[这种鱼]会消失，"一名海洋生物学家说。

pale *adj.* 浅色；（颜色）淡的

biologist *n.* 生物学家

So far, there has been no real effort made to save the coelacanth. People just don't seem to care. "It's [hard] to get money to *conserve* an animal that you can't see, and which tourists can't pay to go and look at," says the biologist. He also notes that people love to save animals that are warm and *furry*. They don't always worry about animals that are wet and slimy.

That could spell doom for the coelacanth. Here is a fish that has survived more than 350 million years on its own. Yet it could be wiped out less than 100 years after its discovery by humans. Then the once "dead" fish really will be dead.

到现在为止，还没有一个真正的拯救腔棘鱼的方法。人们好像并不在意。"[很难]为一种你无法见到的生物采取保护措施，没有旅行者能够花钱去见到它，"一名生物学家说。他也指出人们喜欢拯救那些温暖而且毛茸茸的动物，通常不关心湿淋淋、黏糊糊的动物。

那可能就判了腔棘鱼的死刑。这种鱼自己存活了三亿五千万年，但是在人类发现它们后的100年以内就会灭绝。那么这个曾经"死去"的鱼类就真的会死去了。

---

conserve *v.* 保护   furry *adj.* 毛皮的

The 29, OOO-Foot Plunge

Steve Fossett loved a challenge—any challenge. He had the time, money, and courage to take on even the most daring feats. A *millionaire*, Fossett wasn't about to stay home and count his money.

Over the years he tried just about every *endurance* test. He did not always

Steve Fossett flew more than 15,000 miles in his balloon, the Solo Spirit, before a storm caused him to crash into the ocean east of Australia.

高空坠落

　　斯蒂夫·弗赛特乘坐他的"孤独精神号"热气球飞行了15,000英里，最后一场风暴导致他坠落到澳大利亚东部的海洋中。

　　斯蒂夫·弗赛特喜欢挑战——任何挑战。他有时间、金钱和勇气来进行哪怕是最大胆的壮举。作为一个百万富翁，弗赛特不喜欢待在家里数钱。

　　在那些年里，他尝试了所有的持久力测验。他不是总去赢得一项突破

millionaire　*n.*　百万富翁　　　　　　　endurance　*n.*　持久力

set out to win or break a record. Sometimes he just wanted to prove he could do something. So he swam the English Channel. He raced with a team of dogs across Alaska. He competed in a 24-hour car race and ran in a 100-mile road race. When it came to ocean sailing, Fossett was one of the very best. He set eight long distance records in that sport.

His greatest *challenge*, however, came in the air. Fossett wanted to fly *nonstop* around the world in a hot-air balloon. Others had tried to do this. So far, no one had made it. Weather or other problems always forced the balloonists to land. Fossett himself tried it five times. He never made it. In fact, on one trip he was lucky just to escape with his life.

或者创造新的纪录。有时他只是想证明他能够做到什么事情。所以他游过了英吉利海峡，带了一个狗群通过阿拉斯加，参加了一次24小时的汽车竞赛，并且跑过100英里的公路赛跑。在玩海洋帆船时，弗赛特是最好的运动员之一。在那种运动中他创造了8个长距离的记录。

但是，他的最大的挑战来自于空中。弗赛特打算进行一次没有停歇乘坐热气球的环球旅行。也有其他人试图这样做过，但是没有人成功过。天气或者其他因素经常强迫热气球驾驶员降落。弗赛特自己尝试过5次，也都没有成功。实际上，有一次旅程他差点把命搭上。

---

challenge *n.* 挑战　　　　　　　　　　　　　nonstop *adv.* 不休息地

In 1996, in his first attempt, Fossett traveled only 2,000 miles before he was forced to land. A year later he took off from St. Louis and made it halfway around the world to India. That trip covered more than 10,000 miles. At the time, it set a world record. In his third attempt Fossett again launched from St. Louis. Five days and 6,000 miles later, he came down in a wheat field in Russia. On August 7, 1998, he began his fourth flight. This was the one that almost killed him. For this fourth flight Fossett *launched* his balloon, Solo Spirit, from South America. The 150-foot-high balloon headed east.

At first things went well. Fossett flew over the Atlantic Ocean. He crossed Africa and the Indian Ocean. He crossed Australia in record time. Nine days into the flight, Fossett had logged more than 15,200

1996年，他的第一次尝试中，弗赛特仅仅飞行了2000英里就被迫降落。一年后，他从圣路易斯出发绕了半个地球来到了印度。这个旅程达到了10,000英里。当时，也创造了世界纪录。他第三次尝试再次在圣路易斯出发。5天，6000英里后，他降落在俄罗斯的一片麦田里面。1998年8月7日，他开始进行第四次飞行，这次飞行差点要了他的的命。他从南美起飞，驾驶"孤独精神号"开始飞行。这个150英尺高的气球飞向了东方。

起初，一切正常。弗赛特飞过了大西洋，非洲和印度洋。他以一次创纪录的时间通过了澳大利亚。在飞行的9天里面，弗赛特已经飞过了

---

launch *v.* 使升空

miles. Everything had gone smoothly, and he thought this time he would really make it. When he was just five days from landing where he had started in Argentina, Fossett sent an e-mail message to his control center in St. Louis. "Things look good now," he said. "They'd better. Next land is South America. Cheers, Steve." That was the last message he sent.

About 500 miles east of Australia, Fossett ran into trouble. A line of *thunderstorms* suddenly appeared. He was flying at 29,000 feet. At that height he thought he could fly over the top of the storm. He was wrong. The fierce winds sucked him down into the heart of the storm. Although he was over a warm part of the earth, the temperature that high up was below zero. So it didn't rain; it *hailed*.

15,200英里。所有的事情都很顺利，他认为这次他可以真正地完成计划了。正在他还有5天到达他在阿根廷的出发地点时，弗赛特给位于圣路易斯的控制中心发送了一封电子邮件。"事情看起来很顺利，"他说，"情况很好。下一个土地是南美。庆祝，斯蒂夫。"那是他发送的最后一条信息。

　　在澳大利亚东部500英里处，弗赛特遇到了麻烦。一个雷雨线突然出现了。他飞行在29,000英尺的高度，认为那个高度能够飞过风暴的顶端。他错了，剧烈的风把他吸入风暴的中心。虽然他处于地球的温暖地带，但是高空的气温是在零下的。所以没有下雨，而是下起了冰雹。"大量的冰

---

thunderstorm *n.* 大雷雨　　　　　　　　　　　hail *v.* 下雹

"[There were] *tremendous* sheets of hail just flooding me," Fossett later said. Also, bolts of lightning flashed all around.

Before long, the storm ripped a hole in Fossett's balloon. The Solo Spirit began to fall—fast. Within seconds it was falling at about 30 miles an hour. "I'm going to die," thought Fossett. As he *plummeted*, he kept running the burner full-tilt. It pumped hot air up into the damaged balloon. He knew that wouldn't stop the balloon from falling, but he hoped it would slow it down a bit. Still, it was a fearful *plunge*. "As I was going down," Fossett later said, "the balloon was just being thrown from one side to another."

Half a world away in St. Louis, his support crew knew nothing of Fossett's *predicament*. But they feared the worst. When they lost

---

雹把我淹没了，"后来弗赛特说，而且四周电闪雷鸣。

很快暴风雨就在弗赛特的气球上撕开了一个洞。"孤独精神号"开始快速下降。在几秒钟之内，下降的速度就达到了每小时30英里。"我要死了，"弗赛特想道。在他坠落的过程中，他把火力开到了最大，并把大量的热空气鼓进了破损的气球当中。他知道这样也无法阻止气球下降，但是他希望能够使下降的速度降下来。可是它还是令人恐惧的下降速度。"我正在下降时，"后来弗赛特说，"气球从一边被甩到了另一边。"

在半个世界以外的圣路易斯，他的支持人员对弗赛特遇到的困境一无所知。但是他们害怕最糟糕的情况。当他们同他失去联系时，他们不知道

---

tremendous *adj.* 巨大的
plunge *n.* 猛跌；骤降

plummet *v.* 暴跌；速降
predicament *n.* 困境

contact with him, they didn't know if he was still *aloft*. In fact, they didn't even know if he was still alive. Desperately they kept trying to reach him by radio. "In these situations, you just try to turn off your emotions," said team member Joe Ritchie.

When Fossett's balloon burst, he was over the Coral Sea. That was both a good and a bad place to land. It was good because the warm water was fairly shallow and protected by *coral* reefs, so he would not be tossed about by huge waves. "It's a lot better to [crash in the Coral Sea] than in the open Pacific," said one team member.

The bad part was that the coral reefs in this part of the ocean were uncharted. No one knew exactly where the reefs were. So rescuers ran the risk of hitting one. That could rip out the bottom of a

---

弗赛特是否还在飞行。实际上，他们甚至不知道他是否还活着，只是绝望地想通过无线电联系他。"在那些条件下，你要试着关掉感情，"支持队伍成员乔·里奇说。

当弗赛特的气球爆炸时，他正在珊瑚海的上空。那里既是一个降落的好地点，也是一个坏地点。说它是个好地点是因为那里温暖的海水很浅，而且受到珊瑚礁的保护，所以他不会在巨浪中翻腾。"[在珊瑚海坠毁]比在太平洋的中心坠毁要强得多。"一名队员说。

糟糕的事情是珊瑚海在海图上没有标明。没有人知道这个珊瑚海的确切位置。所以营救人员要冒着触礁的危险。那会撕破船底，而且也是大白

---

aloft *adv.* 在空中高处   coral *n.* 珊瑚

boat. Also, the Coral Sea is home to the great white shark. If Fossett survived the 29,000-foot fall, he might still have to deal with these *fearsome* creatures.

Incredibly, Fossett did survive the fall. However, when he hit the water, he was knocked out. He also suffered small burns on his wrist and nose. When he woke up, Fossett realized that his *capsule* was upside down. Part of it was filling with water. Another part was on fire. Quickly Fossett climbed into a small life *raft* he had carried on board. As he pulled the life raft away from the capsule, the balloon's *propane* gas tanks exploded. Luckily, the blast didn't reach him.

Fossett's emergency beacon sent out a distress signal. That alerted ships and planes that he was in the area. Still, it took awhile

---

鲨的故乡。如果弗赛特从29,000英尺的坠落中幸存了下来，他可能还要对付这些可怕的生物。

令人难以置信的是，弗赛特的确从这次坠落中幸存了下来。但是当他落入水中时，他被撞晕了过去。他的手腕和鼻子有小块的灼伤。当他醒来时，弗赛特意识到他的飞行舱被倒扣了过来。里面的一部分充满了水，另一部分起火了。弗赛特很快就爬到了他在飞机上面带着的一个小救生筏上。当他正在划着筏子远离飞行舱时，热气球的丙烷罐发生了爆炸。幸运的是，爆炸没有伤到他。

弗赛特的紧急信号装置发出了求救信号，通知了船只和飞机他在这个区域。但是一架搜索飞机要用很长时间来找到他的位置。机组人员给他

---

fearsome *adj.* 可怕的
raft *n.* 筏子

capsule *n.* 航天舱
propane *n.* 丙烷

for a search plane to locate him. The crew dropped a larger raft for him to wait in until he could be picked up. At last he was rescued by a ship that was on its own voyage around the world. The captain, Laurie Piper, had heard that Fossett was down and went looking for him. Somehow, she had managed to miss all the reefs while sailing in the dark!

The news that Fossett was safe delighted his team members back in St. Louis. "We've been sweating *bullets* for about eight hours," said one. "So we're feeling pretty good now."

Another agreed. "He is *fortunate*. There are not too many people who have been in a storm like that."

Steve Fossett survived his 29,000-foot plunge, but the Solo Spirit

---

投下了一个大筏子，以便他在上面等候救援队的到来。最后他被一艘船营救，当时这艘船也在进行环球旅行。船长，劳里·皮普听说弗赛特落水，特地前来搜索他。她也不知道在黑暗中是如何避开所有珊瑚礁的！

弗赛特安全的消息使圣路易斯的团队高兴了起来。"我们在极度紧张中度过了8个小时，"一个人说，"所以现在我们感觉好多了。"

另一个人表示同意。"他很幸运。遇到过那样风暴的人并不多。"

斯蒂夫·弗赛特在他29,000英尺的坠落中幸存了下来，但是"孤独精神号"却没有那么幸运。飞行舱严重受损，而且大部分的装备丢失了。这

---

bullet *n.* 子弹　　　　　　　　　　　　　fortunate *adj.* 幸运的

did not *fare* as well. The capsule was badly damaged, and most of the equipment was lost. That ruled out a second try in 1998. Fossett joined forces with another team. But their attempt in December also failed.

Soon there was no need to try anymore. In March 1999 the balloon Breitling Orbiter 3 made a nonstop flight around the world. That trip, made by Brian Jones and Bertrand Piccard, took 19 days. It covered more than 29,000 miles, breaking all the *records* for such a flight. Steve Fossett would have to find a new challenge to test his skill and daring.

使1998年进行另外一次尝试成为不可能。弗赛特参加了另外一个组织的行动。但是他们在12月的尝试也以失败告终。

很快没有必要进行再一次尝试了。在1999年3月"布立特林·奥比特三号"成功地进行了一次不停歇的环球旅行。这次旅行是由布里恩·琼斯和波特兰得·皮卡得用了19天完成的。他们飞行了29,000多英里，打破了这种飞行的所有记录。斯蒂夫·弗赛特只好找一种新的挑战来检验他的技能和胆量了。

---

fare *v.* 进展；成功

record *n.* 记录

12

A Guardian Angel

It was late in the day when Christene Skubish left Placerville, California. She *buckled* her three-year-old son Nicky into the passenger seat of her small red car. Then she set out to visit friends in Carson City, Nevada.

Christene Skubish's car was destroyed when it plunged over the edge of a cliff along a California highway. Miraculously, her son Nicky survived the crash.

守护天使

克里斯蒂·斯库比什的车冲下了加利福尼亚高速公路旁边的悬崖，完全被毁掉了。令人惊奇的是，她的儿子尼奇在这次事故中幸存了下来。

当克里斯蒂·斯库比什离开加利福尼亚的普丽思维尔时天色已晚。她把她三岁大的小儿子用安全带系在她小红车的座椅上。然后出发去拜访居住在内华达州卡森市的朋友们。

---

buckle v. （使）用扣扣住

Sadly, Christene never made it. As she drove along Highway 50 on June 6, 1994, she must have fallen asleep at the wheel. She drove right off the road, leaving no *skid* marks at all. The car rolled 40 feet down a steep bank. It crashed into a thick forest of trees. Nicky was not badly hurt, but Christene was killed instantly.

No one saw the accident take place. So Christene's friends had no idea why she and Nicky didn't arrive in Carson City as planned. For five days no one knew what had happened. During that time Nicky stayed near the body of his dead mother. He didn't know why she wouldn't wake up, but he didn't want to leave her. So even though he *crawled* out of the wrecked car from time to time, he didn't go far, and he eventually returned to the front seat to lie down beside her.

可悲的是，克里斯蒂没能到达那里，1994年6月6日当她在50号高速公路上行驶时，一定是在驾驶时睡着了。她驾车冲出了公路，根本没有留下路面划痕，冲下了一个40英尺的高坡，撞毁在一片浓密的树林里面。尼奇没有受到重伤，但是克里斯蒂马上就死了。

没有人看到这次事故的发生情况。所以克里斯蒂的朋友不知道为什么她和尼奇没有如约到达卡森市。5天以来没有人知道发生了什么事情。在此期间，尼奇待在他死去的母亲身边。他不知道她为什么不能醒过来，但是他不想离开母亲，所以尽管他几次从破损的车里面爬出来，他也没有走远，最后回到了前座那里并在母亲的身边躺了下来。

---

skid *n.* 打滑   crawl *v.* 爬

As the hours passed Nicky became hungry and thirsty. There was no food around for him to eat and nothing at all to drink. During the day the temperature rose into the 90s. Nicky got so hot he took off all his clothes. But at night the temperature *plummeted* back down to about 50 degrees. Because Nicky couldn't manage to get his clothes back on, he lay on the seat naked, shivering with cold. By the fourth night he was so weak he could barely move at all.

Meanwhile, Christene's friends and family were becoming more and more worried. They contacted the El Dorado County Sheriff's Department. Deputy Rich Strasser began to *investigate* but could find no leads.

Then, at 3 A.M. on June 11, a woman named Deborah Hoyt saw a bizarre sight. She and her husband were driving along Highway

---

随着时间的流逝，尼奇变得饥饿而且口渴。他附近没有食物，也没有什么喝的。在白天气温达到（华氏）90度。尼奇感到很热，他脱掉了所有的衣服。但是晚上，气温降到50度。因为尼奇不会自己把衣服穿上，他赤裸着躺在座椅上，冻得瑟瑟发抖。到第四天晚上，他已经很虚弱，以至于根本不能动了。

同时，克里斯蒂的朋友们和家人越来越着急。他们联系了艾尔·多拉多县的警察局。里奇·斯特拉萨警官开始调查这个事件，但是没有线索。

在6月11日凌晨3:00左右，一名叫作德伯拉·郝伊特的妇女看到了一个奇怪的景象。她和她的丈夫旅行归来驾车通过50号公路。她的丈夫驾

---

plummet *v.* 垂直落下   investigate *v.* 调查

50 on their way home from a trip. With her husband at the wheel, Deborah Hoyt was looking out the window. Suddenly she saw a naked woman lying by the side of the road. The woman was *curled* up in a ball, with one arm thrown across her head as though *shielding* her face.

"I just started screaming and screaming," Hoyt said. Her husband hadn't seen the woman, but he agreed they should get help right away. They stopped at a forest ranger's station two miles down the road and called the police.

When the highway police arrived, the Hoyts took them back to the spot where Deborah had seen the woman. There was no one there. The officers searched for an hour, covering a five-mile stretch of Highway 50. But they came up empty.

驶着车，德伯拉·郝伊特向窗外看着。突然她看到路边躺着一个裸体的女人。女人蜷缩成了一团，一只手掩住了她的脸。

　　"我开始尖叫，尖叫，"郝伊特说。她的丈夫没有见到那个妇女，但是他同意他们应该马上寻求帮助。他们在2英里外的护林员住宅停了下来，然后报警。

　　当高速公路的警察到达时，郝伊特夫妇带他们来到了德伯拉看到那个女人的地方，但是什么都没有。警察们搜索了一个小时，整整搜索了50号高速公路上的5英里，可是什么也没有找到。

---

curl v. 蜷缩；卷曲　　　　　　shield v. 保护某人或某物（免遭危险、伤害或不快）

Yet Deborah Hoyt was absolutely certain about what she had seen. So at 5 A.M. that morning the officers put in a call to the El Dorado County Sheriff's office. They asked a local officer to follow up on Hoyt's strange sighting.

When Rich Strasser heard about the naked woman, he immediately thought of Christene Skubish. Deborah Hoyt's *description* of the naked woman matched that of Christene. So Deputy Strasser decided to drive out to Highway 50 himself and have a look around.

When he got out to the area where Hoyt had seen the woman, Strasser slowed down. The sun was just rising, and the road was deserted. As he *crept* along, Strasser saw no sign of a woman anywhere. But suddenly he spotted a small black object lying on the road. It was a child's hightop shoe.

但是德伯拉·郝伊特对于所看到的东西完全确定。所以在早晨5点，警察接通了艾尔·多拉多警察局的电话。他们请当地的警方在郝伊特奇怪的目击情况中参加调查。

当里奇·斯特拉萨听到裸体女性的描述，他马上想起了克里斯蒂·斯库比什。德伯拉·郝伊特对裸体女性的描述还符合克里斯蒂的情况。所以斯特拉萨警官决定开车到50号高速公路那里去看一看。

当他到达郝伊特看到那个女人的地方时，斯特拉萨慢了下来。太阳刚刚升起，路面上没有车。他驾驶着车缓慢前行，没有看到有女人的痕迹。但是他突然发现了路上的一个小的黑色物体，那是一个儿童穿的高筒鞋。

---

description *n.* 描述

creep *v.* 缓慢地行进

Strasser pulled to a stop and jumped out of the car. He looked out over the steep bank. At first he saw nothing. Then, down among the trees, he saw the *smashed* remains of a red car.

With his heart pumping wildly, Strasser slid down the steep bank. He was hoping for a happy ending to the Skubish disappearance. But when he got to the car, he saw Christene's body strapped in her seat. He also saw Nicky curled up beside her, blue and unmoving. It looked as though both of them were dead.

As Strasser bent over Nicky, however, he heard the little boy sigh. Nicky was alive! He couldn't believe Nicky had survived this long *amid* the *wreckage*. In fact, Nicky Skubish was on the verge of death. "He didn't talk or move, just lay there breathing," Strasser remembered. "The doctors who saw Nicky said if I hadn't found him when I did, he would have been dead within an hour."

斯特拉萨马上停下车，跳了下来。他从陡峭的悬崖向下看。起初他什么也没有看到。仔细看了看，他发现在树丛中有一辆红色汽车撞毁的残骸。

斯特拉萨的心跳加快了，他滑下了陡坡，希望斯库比什的失踪是一个快乐的结局。但是当他到达小汽车那里时，发现克里斯蒂的尸体被夹在座椅上，还看到在她身边蜷成一团的尼奇，身上青紫，一动不动。看起来好像两个人都死了。

斯特拉萨弯下腰，仔细检查尼奇，突然他听到小男孩的喘息声。尼奇还活着!他无法相信尼奇在这样的废墟里面幸存了这么久。实际上，尼奇·斯库比什在死亡的边缘。"他不能说话，也不能动，就是在那里喘气，"斯特拉萨回忆道，"看到尼奇的医生们说，如果我当时没有找到他，他可能在一个小时之内就会死亡。"

---

smash *v.* 粉碎；破碎
wreckage *n.* 废墟

amid *prep.* 在……之中

After Nicky was rushed to the hospital, Strasser and others tried to piece together what had happened. But some of the facts simply did not make sense. Deborah Hoyt had seen a naked woman by the side of the road. But that woman could not have been Christene Skubish. Investigators were sure she had died in the crash. There were many deep cuts on her body that would have bled heavily. Very little blood had flowed out of these wounds, however, indicating that she had died instantly.

Besides, when Strasser found Christene, she was still in the driver's seat of her car with the seatbelt fastened. It didn't make sense to think that Christene had taken her clothes off, scrambled up the bank, *collapsed* by the side of the road, and then slid back down the bank, put her clothes back on, and buckled herself back into her seat before dying.

当尼奇被送到医院后，斯特拉萨和其他人尽量把这个故事拼凑起来。但是其中的一些事实好像毫无意义。德伯拉·郝伊特曾经在路边看到一个赤裸的女人。但是她不可能是克里斯蒂·斯库比什。调查人员确信她在事故中丧生，并且身上有许多很深的创伤，这可能导致她严重出血。但是这些伤口仅仅流出了很少的血，表明她马上就死了。

而且当斯特拉萨找到克里斯蒂时，她还在驾驶员的座椅上，安全带系得很牢固。如果说，克里斯蒂脱下了衣服，爬上了陡坡，在路边倒下，又滑回了陡坡下，然后再穿上衣服，爬回座椅，系好安全带，死去，这简直就是天方夜谭。

---

collapse *v.* 倒下；坍陷

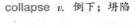

The naked person could not have been Nicky, either. "A healthy person would have had a very difficult time climbing up that *embankment*," said Strasser. "By the time Deborah Hoyt had seen someone, Nicky would have been too weak to move."

Then there was the matter of the black hightop shoe. No one could explain how it ended up in the middle of the road. If it had been there since the crash, why didn't the highway police officers find it when they searched the area? If Nicky had somehow managed to climb up the bank, it didn't make sense that he would carry one shoe up with him, drop the shoe in the middle of the road, and then slide down the bank again.

Finally, there were questions raised about Christene Skubish's body. It had not *decayed* at all. A body that had sat in 90-degree heat for five days should have been smelly and rotten. But

---

那个赤裸的人也不可能是尼奇。"一个健康的人也很难爬上那个陡坡，"斯特拉萨说，"当德伯拉·郝伊特看到什么人时，尼奇可能太虚弱了以至于根本无法动弹。"

然后还有那个黑色高筒鞋的问题。没有人能够解释它是怎么到的道路中央。如果事故发生时就在那里，那么高速公路警察搜索时为什么没有发现它呢？如果尼奇不知怎样爬上了陡坡，他带着一只鞋，放到路中央，然后再回来也是不可能的。

最后关于克里斯蒂·斯库比什的尸体也存在着问题。它完全没有腐烂。一个在90度的高温下存放5天的尸体应该发出气味，并且腐烂。但是克里斯蒂的尸体却完好。实际上，营救人员发现它上面有一种甜蜜的气

---

embankment *n.* （公路或铁路两侧的）护坡；路基　　　　decay *v.* 腐烂；变质

Christene's body was in perfect shape. In fact, rescue workers noted a sweet smell surrounding it. "It's almost as though the condition of her body was preserved to make things easier for her son," mused Strasser. "In his mind, he thought his mom was just asleep."

In the end some people concluded that the naked woman was an *angel*. They said Nicky's guardian angel was guiding rescuers to his side. Others thought it was the *spirit* of Christene Skubish making one last attempt to save her son. But whoever or whatever it was, it saved the life of Nicky Skubish. If Deborah Hoyt had not seen the naked woman by the side of the road and gone for help, Nicky Skubish would not be alive today.

味。"好像她身体的情况就是要保存下来为她的儿子更好地生存下去，"斯特拉萨思索着说，"在他的意识里，他认为他的妈妈就是睡着了。"

最后一些人下结论说，那个裸体的女人就是个天使。尼奇的保护天使把救援人员引导到了他的身边。另一些人认为是克里斯蒂·斯库比什的灵魂做出最后努力来拯救她的孩子。但是无论她是谁，是什么东西，她都拯救了尼奇·斯库比什的生命。如果德伯拉·郝伊特没有在路边看到一个赤裸的女人而去寻求帮助，尼奇·斯库比什今天就不会活着了。

---

angel *n.* 天使   spirit *n.* 灵魂

13

A Shocking Experience

It could happen to you almost anywhere. You could be walking along the golf course. You could be enjoying an outdoor picnic or *sailing* on the open water. It could also happen as you talk on the phone, wash the dishes, or even as you watch TV. But the odds are very much

Although the odds are against it, people can be struck by lightning just about anywhere.

电打雷劈

虽然概率很小但是人们可能在任何地方受到雷击。

哪里都有可能发生。你可能是走在高尔夫球场上，你可能是在享用一次室外的野餐或者在开阔的水面上航海。也许你在打电话，刷洗盘子，或者甚至在看电视。但是这种事情发生的概率真的是太小了，只有六十万分之一的人才有可能被雷电击中。

sail v. 航行

against it. Only one person in about 600,000 ever gets struck by lightning.

Given those numbers, you'd have to call any lightning victim unlucky. But what do you call a person who has been hit seven times? *Incredibly* unlucky? That hardly seems strong enough. But you'd have to call Roy Sullivan something. Between 1942 and 1977, he was struck by lightning seven times. That is a world record.

Sullivan worked as a park ranger in Virginia. His first encounter with lightning cost him a big toe. Later hits *scorched* his eyebrows, *singed* his hair, and burned his shoulder. In 1973 Sullivan suffered the worst hit of his life. He was stepping out of his truck when lightning streaked toward him. "It set my hat and hair on fire," he later said.

获得了这个数字你可能会称任何雷电击中的受害者运气太差。但是如果这个人被雷电击中7次你又会怎么说？太不幸了？看起来没有什么力度来证明。但是你的确要称洛伊·苏列文点什么了。在1942年至1977年之间，他被雷电击中7次，这也是个世界纪录。

苏列文在弗吉尼亚的一个公园里面做看守员。他第一次与雷电偶遇要了他的一个大脚趾，后来的几次雷击烧焦了他的眉毛，烤煳了他的头发，烧伤了他的肩膀。1973年，苏列文遭到了他一生中最严重的一次雷击。当时他正从卡车上下来，突然一道闪电出现在他的头上。"它把我的帽子

---

incredibly *adv.* 非常　　　　　　　　　　　　　　　　scorch *v.* 烤焦
singe *v.* 烧焦

"Then it went down my left arm and leg, knocked off my shoe, and crossed over to my right leg. It also set my underwear on fire."

Despite Sullivan's record, Virginia is not the state with the most lightning. That distinction belongs to Florida. The peninsula of Florida lies between two warm bodies of water. High *humidity* and hot weather breed many violent storms. It is really bad during the hottest time of the year. That's when the "Sunshine State" gets *bombarded* with thunderstorms and lightning. About 5 million bolts of lightning strike Florida each year. That is far more than in any other state.

Lightning kills people every year. But it also does some strange things to people who get hit and somehow live. Take the case of Florida's George McBay. One day in 1993 he was helping to lower a

---

和头发点着了，"后来他说，"然后它通过了我的左胳膊和左腿，毁掉了我的鞋，而且也穿过了我的右腿，它也把我的内衣点着了。"

尽管苏列文的记录惊人，但是弗吉尼亚州并不是一个雷电最多的州。这个殊荣应当属于佛罗里达。佛罗里达半岛位于两大温暖水域之间。高湿度和炎热的天气导致了许多剧烈的风暴。在一年的最炎热时期这是很厉害的，这时"阳光州"就会被雷雨和闪电所席卷。每年在佛罗里达大约发生五百万次雷电。这比其他任何的州都要多。

每年，雷电都会杀死人。但是经常发生一些奇怪的事情，就是有些人被击中但是却活了下来。比如佛罗里达的乔治·麦克贝。1993年的一

---

humidity n. 湿度

bombard v. 轰炸；轰击

large metal pipe from a roof. Suddenly, he was struck by lightning. "It felt like everything in my body just blew out the top of my head," he said.

The lightning bolt didn't kill McBay. But it changed his life forever. "The best day that I've had since the accident isn't as good as the worst day I had before the accident," McBay later said. "You get lost. Blackouts. A good day is lying on the *couch*."

Sherri Spain could *sympathize* with McBay. On August 27, 1989, Spain was in Maryville, Tennessee. She and her volleyball team were taking a lunch break outside a gym. As they ate, a storm rolled in. Spain really liked storms. She liked the crack of thunder and the flash of lightning. "My heart races during a storm," she once said.

天，他正在帮忙把一个金属管道从房顶上取下来，突然他被雷电击中了。"我感觉我体内所有东西都从我的头上冲了出去，"他说。

这次雷击并没有击毙麦克贝，但是它永远地改变了他的一生。"受到雷击后我过得最好的一天，都不如事前最坏的一天。"后来麦克贝说，"你会出现失忆，眩晕。最好的就是一天躺在沙发上。"

夏利·斯佩恩应当和麦克贝有同感。1989年8月27日，斯佩恩在田纳西的马里维尔，她的排球队在体育馆外进行午餐休息。他们正在用餐，一场暴风雨出现了。斯佩恩很喜欢风暴，她喜欢打雷的声音和看到闪电。

---

couch n. 长沙发　　　　　　　　　　　　sympathize v. 同情；支持

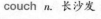

So when the wind began to blow and the rain came, Spain stood just outside the gym with Dawn Platt, one of her students. All the other students ran for cover back inside the gym. "It was stupid," she later admitted.

A lightning *bolt* hit the steel door directly behind Spain and entered the back of her head. She *slumped* to the ground. Platt knelt beside her, not knowing what to do. "I held her hand and called her name, but she didn't respond," Platt later recalled. "I thought she was dead. All I could do was scream for help and pray."

Spain lived, but the lightning affected her in many ways. She lost sight in her right eye and hearing in her right ear. Her hair, which had been dark brown, turned *blonde*. She developed heart trouble. Spain

---

"在风暴中，我的心也跟着驰骋，"一次她这样说。

所以当风开始吹，雨开始下时，斯佩恩就站在体育馆的外面，旁边是她的一个学生，道恩·普赖特。所有其他学生都跑回了体育馆去避雨。"那个行动太蠢了，"她后来承认着。

一道闪电击中了斯佩恩后面的一道金属门，进入她的后脑。她被击倒在地上。普赖特跪在她的身旁，不知道该怎么办。"我抓住了她的手，喊着她的名字，但是她没有反应，"后来普赖特回忆道，"我以为她死了，我所能做的就是大喊救命而且祈祷。"

斯佩恩幸存了下来，但是闪电在多个方面影响了她。她的右眼和右耳失去功能。头发原来是深棕色的，现在变成了金黄色。她也出现了心脏

---

bolt *n.* 闪电
blonde *adj.* 金黄色的

slump *v.* 重重地坐下（或倒下）

also lost much of her brain power. As a teacher, Spain had always valued her mental *abilities*. Yet suddenly she couldn't even remember the letters of the alphabet. It took her a year of *grueling* work to rebuild her basic skills. Even then she still had memory problems. She couldn't remember facts or dates. When she finally returned to the classroom, Spain spent hours each night preparing her lessons and had to use lots of notes.

It may seem hard to believe, but once in a great while being struck by lightning can be a *blessing*. In February 1971 Edwin Robinson lost control of his truck and crashed on an icy road in Maine. His head went through the back window. As a result, he suffered brain damage. Slowly, he lost his sight and much of his hearing. He had to

---

疾病，大脑功能也失去了许多。作为教师，斯佩恩需要她的精神能力。但是突然之间她就连简单的字母表也无法记住。她花费了一年的艰辛努力来重新建立基本的技能。即使这样，她的记忆力还是存在问题，她无法记忆事实和日期。当她重返课堂时，每天晚上要花费几个小时的时间来准备课程，还要使用很多笔记。

人们听起来可能难以置信，但那是真的，被雷电击中也许是个好事。在1971年2月，艾得文·洛宾森驾驶卡车失去控制在缅因州结冰的路面上发生事故。他的头撞破了后车窗，结果是他的大脑受伤。他渐渐地失去了视

---

ability *n.* 能力
blessing *n.* 好事

grueling *adj.* 使人筋疲力尽的

learn Braille and wear a hearing aid. Robinson lived this way for nine years.

Then, on June 4, 1980, Robinson went for a short walk in the rain with his *aluminum* cane. Without warning, a bolt of lightning hit him and knocked him out. For 20 minutes, he lay unconscious on the ground. At last he woke up and returned to his house. He felt very tired, but otherwise he seemed fine. He decided to take a nap.

Then something *remarkable* happened. When he woke up from his nap, he could read the time on the kitchen clock. He hadn't been able to do that for nine years. Within a few days, he could see well enough to walk without a cane. His hearing also improved greatly. He even began to *regrow* some hair on his bald head.

觉和大部分听力，他要学习盲文和佩戴助听器。洛宾森这样生活了9年。

1980年6月4日，洛宾森带着他的铝制手杖在雨中作短暂的散步。在毫无预兆的情况下，一道闪电击中了他，使他昏厥过去。近20分钟，他躺在地上毫无知觉。最后他醒了过来，然后回到了家里。他感到十分劳累，但是其他的情况都很正常。他决定小睡一会。

然后发生了不寻常的转变。当他睡醒时，他能够看得清厨房上时钟的时间。已经9年了，他无法做这样简单的事情。几天之内，他能够看清楚许多东西，而不用使用拐杖了。他的听力也获得了极大的提高，甚至他的

---

aluminum *n.* 铝
regrow *v.* 再生长

remarkable *adj.* 不寻常的；显著的

Edwin Robinson's case is a rare exception. You don't want to test your luck by running around in a thunderstorm waving a golf club over your head. You should always treat lightning for what it is—a potential killer. Hurricanes and *tornadoes* make the news because they tend to kill in large numbers. Lightning picks off its victims one at a time. In the end, though, lightning kills more Americans than almost any other weather *hazard*.

The odds of getting struck by a bolt of lightning are still about as high as winning the *lottery*. But unlike the lottery, looking for lightning bolts is a game most people would rather not play.

秃顶上也重新长出了一些头发。

艾得文·洛宾森的事件是一次少见的特例。你可不要在雷雨天四处乱跑，在头上挥舞着高尔夫球棒。你应该总是把闪电看成它真正的角色——一个潜在的杀手。飓风和龙卷风是新闻的中心，因为它们总是大规模地夺走人们的生命。雷电一次会夺走一个人的生命。但是最终，雷电几乎比其他任何天气灾难致死的人都要多。

被雷电击中的概率仍然像赢得一场彩票一样。但是不像彩票游戏，寻找雷电大部分人可是不喜欢做的。

---

tornado *n.* 龙卷风　　　　　　　　　　hazard *n.* 危险；危害
lottery *n.* 彩票

14

Crocker Land: An Arctic Mirage

Robert Peary picked up his *binoculars* and looked toward the northwest. What he saw made his heart leap. On the far *horizon* he spotted a vast, snow-capped mountain range. It was something that didn't appear on any maps. "I looked longingly at this land,"

Arctic mirages such as this are caused by a special mix of air that bends light.

科洛克地：北极的海市蜃楼

像这样的北极海市蜃楼是由于空气的特殊混合折射光而导致的。

罗伯特·皮里拿起了双筒望远镜，向西北方向看。他看到的东西使他的心脏加速跳动起来。在远方的地平线上，他发现了一个宽阔的，上面有冰雪覆盖的山脉，这是地图上没有标出的。"我渴望地看着这片土地，"

---

binocular *n.* 双筒望远镜　　　　　　　　　　horizon *n.* 地平线

Peary wrote. He saw himself walking along its shores and climbing its mountains. But Peary wasn't prepared to do it on this trip.

The year was 1906. Robert Peary was on his way home. He had been exploring the *polar* area in far northern Canada. At the moment he was standing on Cape Thomas Hubbard at the tip of Axel Heiberg Land. He figured the land he saw was about 120 miles away. Peary built a *cairn*, or pile of rocks, to mark where he stood. Then he decided on a name for the faraway mountain range. He called it Crocker Land in honor of a man who had helped pay for this polar trip.

When Peary got back to America, he told people what he had seen. The image of Crocker Land fired people's imaginations. Some thought it might be a lost island continent. They thought it might

---

皮里写道。他很想到它的海岸走一走，然后爬上它的山峰。但是皮里这次旅行没有打算这样做。

这一年是1906年，罗伯特·皮里正在回家的路上，他探索了加拿大北部的极地地区。当时他正站在埃克塞尔·海博格地的托马斯·胡巴德角上，估计看到的陆地大概有120英里远。皮里建立了一个石堆标记，也就是一堆石头，来标记他所站的地点。然后他为远方的山脉考虑了一个名字，把它叫作科洛克地，来纪念赞助他进行极地旅行的人。

当皮里回到美国时，他告诉了人们他的所见。科洛克地的景象点燃了人们的想象力。一些人认为可能是一座未被人知的大陆。他们认为那上面

---

polar *adj.* 极地的　　　　　　　　　　　　cairn *n.* 堆石标

hold great *treasures* of gold and iron *ore*. Others thought it would turn out to be unfrozen land filled with exciting new forms of life. They pictured it heated by underground "*furnaces*." People pointed out that Inuits talked of a distant land warmed by the sun and filled with herds of animals. Said one man, "If there be an ice-cooled desert, why not a steam-heated polar *paradise*?"

But where exactly was this unmapped land? The American Museum of Natural History decided to find out. In 1913 it sent an expedition to find Crocker Land. The search was led by Donald MacMillan, who had been a member of Peary's last polar expedition. Fitzhugh Green was second in command. That July they headed north. They ran into trouble all along the way. Some of their sled dogs died. The snow was so loose they could not build good igloos.

可能有大量的黄金珍宝和铁矿石，另一些人认为那上面可能是没有冰封的世界而且充满了新的生活方式。他们描绘这个大陆被地下的"熔炉"所加热。人们指出因纽特人曾经谈论过远方的被太阳照耀、上面布满大群野兽的土地。一个人说："如果有冰凉的沙漠怎么就不能有蒸气加热的极地天堂？"

但是这个地图上没有标识的土地到底在哪里？美国国家自然历史博物馆决定找出来。1913年，它派了一个远征队去探索科洛克地。这次搜索是由唐纳德·麦克米兰领导的，他曾经参加过皮里的最后极地探险活动。费佐格·格林是第二指挥。那一年的7月他们向北方进发，但整个行程一直不顺利。他们的一些雪橇狗死了。雪太松，他们无法盖圆顶雪屋。几名

---

treasure n. 金银财宝；珠宝

furnace n. 熔炉

ore n. 矿石

paradise n. 天堂

Several Inuits who joined them got sick with *mumps* and flu. Winter temperatures dropped as low as 50 degrees below zero. Trying to keep warm one night, MacMillan set fire to his sleeping bag by mistake. "I was warm at last," he joked in his journal.

On April 13, 1914, they finally reached Cape Thomas Hubbard. At least, they thought it was the cape. MacMillan and Green searched for the cairn Peary had left eight years before. They couldn't find it. They looked through their binoculars, hoping to get heir first *glimpse* of Crocker Land. They saw nothing but an endless sea of white. Undaunted, they decided to head northwest across the frozen sea anyway. They planned to keep going until they reached Crocker Land.

A little way out they looked back and saw they had missed the

---

参加他们队伍的因纽特人得了腮腺炎和流感。冬季的气温降到了零下50度。一天晚上为了保暖，麦克米兰无意中把自己的睡袋点着了。"我终于获得了温暖，"他在记录中这样写道。

1914年4月13日，他们最后到达了托马斯·胡巴德角。至少他们认为这里就是那个海角。麦克米兰和格林寻找皮里8年前留下的石堆标识，但是他们没有找到。他们用望远镜进行展望，希望能够获得一点点科洛克地的线索，可什么都没有看到，只是无尽的白色海洋。他们没有沮丧，决定向西北方向无论如何也要穿过冰封的海洋。他们计划一直前进直到到达科洛克地。

前进了一会，他们向后看，已经错过了海角几英里的距离，那没有关

---

mumps *n.* 腮腺炎

glimpse *n.* 一瞥；一看

cape by a few miles. That didn't matter. MacMillan and Green knew where they were, and they knew Crocker Land was just 120 miles away.

As they continued, the expedition again ran into difficulties. The biggest problem was leads, or stretches of open water. These leads were impossible to cross. Usually, a good cold night would do the trick. Still, it was dangerous to cross freshly frozen water. At one point several sled dogs broke through the new ice. Luckily, they were pulled out before shifting *chunks* of ice could crush them.

At last, on the morning of April 21, Green shouted to MacMillan, who was still in his *igloo*. Green said he could see Crocker Land. MacMillan climbed to the peak of a nearby iceberg. "Sure enough!" he wrote in his journal. "There it was as plain as day—hills, valleys,

---

系。麦克米兰和格林知道他们是在哪里，他们知道科洛克地位于大约120英里以外。

随着他们的前进，他们开始遇到困难。最大的困难就是水脉，也就是一段露出的没有封冻的水面。这些水脉是不可能通过的。通常情况是在一个很寒冷的夜晚可以完成这个工作，但是在新冻上的冰面上通行也是危险的。在一个地方有几条雪橇狗掉进了新冻上的冰里面。幸运的是，在飘动的冰块把它们压死之前，就被拉了上来。

最后在4月21日的早晨，格林喊还在冰屋里面的麦克米兰。格林说他可以看到科洛克地了。麦克米兰爬到了附近冰山的顶峰。"的确！"他在记录中写道，"太清晰了——小山、峡谷和冰盖，一块巨大的陆地在延

---

chunk *n.* 厚块；大块　　　　　　　　　　　igloo *n.* 雪屋；冰屋

and ice cap, a *tremendous* land stretching ... [across] the horizon."

But as the group moved closer to Crocker Land, a strange thing happened. The land seemed to move away from them. When they stopped, the land stopped. When they moved again, the land *receded* again. Also, the distant land seemed to change shape. MacMillan wrote, "As we watched it more narrowly its appearance slowly changed."

As evening approached Crocker Land faded from view. The next day, they marched toward it again. "On this day there was the same appearance of land in the west," wrote MacMillan. "But it gradually faded away towards evening."

By April 23 the Inuits were growing restless. They began to drop

---

伸……[在]天边。"

　　但是当整个队伍向科洛克地前进时，奇怪的事情发生了。这块陆地好像是在做远离他们的运动。他们停下来，陆地也停下来。他们前进，陆地也前进。而且远方的陆地好像也在改变着形状。麦克米兰写道："随着我们更加仔细地观察那块土地，我们发现它的外观发生着细微的变化。"

　　随着夜幕降临，科洛克地从视野中消失了。第二天，他们又向它进发了。"今天，西面的土地出现了相同的外观，"麦克米兰写道，"但是在邻近傍晚时，它又逐渐消失了。"

　　到4月23日时，因纽特人们开始不安静起来。他们开始显露出要回家

---

tremendous *adj.* 巨大的　　　　　　　　　　recede *v.* 渐渐后退

hints about going home. Some *scoffed* that Crocker Land was nothing but *mist* in the sky. MacMillan did not want to hear this. He took out his map and showed it to them. The map had a brown spot where Crocker Land was supposed to be. MacMillan said he was not going to turn back until he reached it.

So the group pushed ahead. Green, however, stayed behind to take some *measurements*. Later that day, Green caught up with MacMillan. He showed him what he had learned. They were now 150 miles due northwest from Cape Thomas Hubbard. Yet Peary had said that Crocker Land was only 120 miles from the cape.

The news hit MacMillan hard. He suddenly realized that there must not be a Crocker Land after all. He later wrote, "We had not

---

的暗示。一些人嘲弄地说科洛克地根本不存在，就是在空中的雾气形成的。麦克米兰不想听到这些，他拿出了地图给他们看。地图上的一块棕色的地域就是设想中这块陆地的位置。麦克米兰说他在到达指定位置前不打算回去。

这样这个队伍继续前进。但是格林在后面作了一些测量。那一天的晚些时候，格林赶上了麦克米兰的队伍。他告诉了他找到的结果，他们现在已经从托马斯·胡巴德角向西北前进了150英里。但是皮里说科洛克地距离那个海角只有120英里。

这个消息沉重地打击了麦克米兰。他突然意识到一定没有什么科洛克地。他后来写道："我们不仅到达了地图标记的棕色区域，而且[多走

---

hint *n.* 暗示

mist *n.* 薄雾；水汽

scoff *v.* 嘲笑

measurement *n.* 测量

only reached the brown spot on the map, but were 30 miles [past it]. We scanned every foot of that horizon. [There was] nothing in sight." There were no valleys, no mountains, no land at all. There was nothing but a vast sheet of ice in all directions.

The *expedition* had been chasing a *mirage*. The valleys and mountains they "saw" were just a trick played on them by the forces of nature. Such *illusions* are caused by a special mix of air that bends light. It was like seeing a pool of water on a dry road. In the Arctic, these illusions can appear on a grand scale. An iceberg can look like a city.

Crestfallen, the explorers turned toward home. On April 28 they reached Cape Thomas Hubbard. This time MacMillan and Green

---

了]30英里。我们仔细搜索了天边，什么都没有。"没有山谷，没有群山，根本就没有土地。什么都没有，在各个方向只有无尽的冰雪。

整个远征都是在追索着一个海市蜃楼。他们"见到"的山谷、群山仅仅是自然力量在他们身上开的玩笑。这些幻象是由各种气体的特殊比例混合折射光导致的，这与在干旱的道路上看到一潭清水的原因是一样的。在北极这样的幻象能够以一个大规模出现，一座冰山看起来能够像一座城市。

探险者们垂头丧气地返回了。4月28日，他们到达了托马斯·胡巴德角。这次麦克米兰和格林发现了皮里留下的石堆标记。也就是说，他们就

---

expedition *n.* 远征
illusion *n.* 幻想

mirage *n.* 海市蜃楼

found the cairn left by Peary. That meant they were standing on the very *spot* where Peary first saw Crocker Land. The two men looked out at the horizon. And what did they see? "There was land everywhere," wrote Donald MacMillan. "Had we not just come from far over the horizon, we would have returned to our country and reported land as Peary did."

A few years later planes flew over the whole area. They proved beyond all *doubt* that no Crocker Land existed. The top of the world hid no lost continent, no heated paradise. There was just ice, ice, and more ice.

站在皮里第一次见到科洛克地的准确地点。两个人向天边展望，他们看到了什么呢？"到处都是土地，"唐纳德·麦克米兰写道，"如果我们不是刚刚从远方回来，我们也会回国报告发现一片土地，就像皮里做的那样。"

一些年后，飞机飞过了整个这片地区。它们证明毫无疑问的是科洛克地根本就不存在。世界的顶端没有未发现的大陆，没有暖和的天堂。那里只有冰雪、冰雪和更多的冰雪。"

---

spot *n.* 地点   doubt *n.* 怀疑

15

Fish Killer

"I was *disoriented*" said Dr. JoAnn Burkholder, a scientist at North Carolina State University. "I had burning eyes. I couldn't remember how to dial a telephone number. I couldn't write. It was all very frightening."

Burkholder knew what was

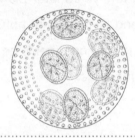

When Pfiesteria attacks, millions of dead fish wash ashore. Sometimes there are so many that bulldozers are needed to remove them.

鱼类谋杀者

当幽灵藻袭击时，数以百万的死亡鱼类被冲到岸边。有时死鱼太多了，需要用推土机来清除它们。

"我彻底地失去了方向感，"乔安·伯克霍德博士说。她是北卡罗莱那州立大学的科学家。"我的眼睛刺痛，我无法记起如何拨电话号码。我不能写，我的状况非常可怕。"

伯克霍德知道是什么导致了这些奇怪的症状。毕竟她是第一个发现事故原因的人之一。

disorient *v.* 使迷路；使迷失方向

causing these strange *symptoms*. After all, she was the one who first discovered the *culprit*.

Her problems were caused by a bizarre member of the *algae* family. It is a microbe so small it has just one cell. Burkholder named it Pfiesteria piscicida. That is Latin for "fish killer".

Burkholder first came across this microbe in 1989. A fellow scientist was having trouble with some *laboratory* fish. The fish kept dying. Burkholder took a careful look at them. She discovered that they were being attacked by the Pfiesteria microbe.

Two years later Burkholder was running more tests on the microbe. She did not think she was doing anything dangerous. But it turned out Pfiesteria could give off deadly fumes. Burkholder breathed in those fumes. That's when she grew sick and confused. Her research aide also grew ill. He had to crawl out of the lab on his

---

她的问题是由一种奇怪的藻类家族成员导致的。这种微生物非常小，仅有一个细胞，伯克霍德称其为"幽灵藻"。用拉丁语说就是"鱼类谋杀者"。

伯克霍德第一次接触到这种微生物是在1989年。一个科研人员在养实验室的鱼的时候遇到了困难，鱼一直在死。伯克霍德仔细地看了看它们，发现它们是被鲨鱼的微生物袭击的结果。

两年后，伯克霍德在这种微生物上进行了更多的实验。她并不认为她在进行什么危险的行动。但是后来证明幽灵藻能够释放出致命的毒气。伯克霍德吸入了这些毒气，这样她就生病了，并且出现困惑。她的实验助理也出现了疾病，他要用手和膝盖爬出实验室，他用了几个月才恢复过来。

---

symptom *n.* 症状
algae *n.* 藻；海藻

culprit *n.* 罪犯；肇事者
laboratory *n.* 实验室

hands and knees. It took him months to recover.

The lab wasn't the only place the microbe was causing trouble. In 1991, huge numbers of fish suddenly began dying in North Carolina's Pamlico Sound. Burkholder *suspected* Pfiesteria was to blame. She was right. The microbe was poisoning, then eating, the fish. Since then there have been other fish kills in the state. There have also been fish kills in Virginia and Maryland.

How could such a tiny creature do so much damage? In fact, most of the time the microbe doesn't do any damage at all. It lives in small numbers in the mud at the mouths of rivers. Mostly it feeds on *bacteria* and other algae and stays out of trouble. That's why no one even knew it was a threat until 1991.

But under just the right conditions, the microbe earns its nickname of "the cell from hell." It multiplies or "blooms" very fast. It swells in

---

实验室不是这种微生物唯一导致问题的地方。1991年，在北卡罗莱那的帕姆力克·松德地区出现大量的鱼类突然死亡。伯克霍德怀疑罪魁祸首是幽灵藻。她是正确的。这种微生物首先毒杀了鱼类，然后吃掉了鱼类。从那时起，州里也出现了其他的鱼类死亡情况，在弗吉尼亚和马里兰也出现了鱼类死亡的情况。

这样一种微小的生物怎么导致了这么多的破坏呢？实际上，大多数的时候这种微生物根本不起破坏作用。它们少量地生存在河口地带的淤泥里面。大多数的情况是它们靠细菌和其他藻类为食，不制造麻烦。这就是为什么在1991年前没有人知道它还是个威胁。

但是在适当的条件下，这种微生物就获得了"地狱细胞"的绰号。它

---

suspect *v.* 怀疑   bacteria *n.* 细菌

size. It begins to show both plant and animal features. Amazingly, the microbe can change into 24 different shapes. No other known creature can do that. It changes shape depending on what it plans to eat.

When fish is on the menu, Pfiesteria grows two little tails. It uses these to swim toward its prey. Drawing near, it shoots a deadly poison or *toxin* into the water. This toxin stuns all fish in the area. The fish become dazed and confused. They begin to *gasp* for oxygen. They start swimming upside down or in circles. As they die, the microbe moves in to eat their flesh.

Pfiesteria often goes years without causing any harm. When the microbe does bloom, it is usually between April and October. Also, the blooms only occur in certain spots. The microbe is not found

---

们复制或者说"生长"得很快，大小也发生了变化。它们开始展示出植物和动物的特征。令人惊奇的是，这种微生物能够变成24种不同的形状，没有任何一种已知的生物能够做到这样。它们形状的改变取决于要吃什么。

如果要吃鱼，幽灵藻就长出两条小尾巴，使用它们游向猎物。当距离很近时，它就向水中射出致命的毒素。这种毒素会镇住这里所有的鱼。鱼类开始晕眩，它们开始大口地呼吸氧气，并开始上下游动或者转圈游动。等到它们死后，这种微生物就会进入鱼体内，去吃它们的肉。

幽灵藻可以存活多年而不导致危害。当这种微生物大量繁殖时，经常是在4月和10月间。而且这种大繁殖只是出现在特定的地点。这种生物没

---

toxin *n.* 毒素

gasp *v.* 喘气

in the open ocean or in rivers far from the coast. It only lives where the fresh water of a river meets the salt water of the sea. In these spots the water moves slowly. That makes it the perfect home for Pfiesteria.

Most importantly, perhaps, the microbe only *blooms* when there are a lot of fish around. It may be that the fish themselves give off some chemical that wakes up the Pfiesteria. Or perhaps water pollution does the trick. Fertilizers or animal waste from nearby farms could be to blame. These *substances* often attract large numbers of fish. But they might also cause the Pfiesteria to bloom.

While no one really knows what causes the microbe to attack, scientists agree that the results are *gruesome*. Fishermen are often

---

有在大海里面或者远离海岸的河流中发现。它只存活在淡水和海洋的咸水相遇的地方。这些地点，水流缓慢，这使之成为幽灵藻的最佳栖息地。

也许最重要的是，当附近鱼类很多时，这种微生物突然旺盛起来。也许是鱼类自己放出的某种化学物质激发了幽灵藻。或者也许是水体的污染导致的后果。化肥和附近农场的动物性废物是罪魁祸首，这些物质经常吸引了大量的鱼，但是也有可能是它们导致幽灵藻旺盛发展起来。

但是没有人知道是什么导致了幽灵藻的袭击，科学家们认为结果是可怕的。经常是渔民第一个发现这种攻击。他们开始发现水中出现一些身上

---

bloom *v.* 旺盛　　　　　　　　　　　　　　　substance *n.* 物质
gruesome *adj.* 可怕的

the first to spot an attack. They begin to see fish with red open *sores* all over their bodies. A short while later, millions of dead fish wash ashore. Workers need *bulldozers* to get rid of all the dead bodies. Seeing such a fish kill is not fun. River officials in North Carolina know how bad it can be. "We had some folks on the boat with us [who] were seeing [a fish kill] for the first time," said one. "These were grown men. They were actually crying."

Then there is the danger to humans. After all, fumes from the microbe made Dr. Burkholder and her aide sick. Couldn't they do the same to other people? "I think Pfiesteria should be taken very seriously," Burkholder said in 1997. She believes the microbe could be a serious health problem.

有红色伤口的死鱼，不一会，数以百万的死鱼就被冲到了岸上，工人们甚至需要用推土机来清除这些死鱼。看到这样的鱼类死亡可一点也不好玩。在北卡罗莱那的河流官员们知道这有多么糟糕。"我们船上有一些人是第一次看到鱼类死亡的事件，"一个人说，"他们都是成年人，忍不住都哭了起来。"

然后，还有对人类的危险。毕竟这种微生物的气体导致伯克霍德博士和她的助手得病。它们对于其他人是不是也会产生这样的后果呢？"我认为幽灵藻应该认真对待，"1997年伯克霍德说。她认为这种微生物可能导致一种严重的健康问题。

---

sore *n.* 痛处；伤处　　　　　　　　bulldozer *n.* 推土机

Others disagree. North Carolina's health director is not convinced that Pfiesteria is a *threat* to humans. Still, he has praised Burkholder's work and called her "an outstanding scientist." He knows that people have many questions about Pfiesteria. "We want to know the answers," he said.

Some things are already known. The microbe is not going to cause the next *plague*. Scientists say that it can't be "caught" like a cold or flu. Still, it can be dangerous for anyone who is around when the toxin is shot out. It is not wise to be in the water at such a time. Scientists say that breathing the fumes from the toxin can also be harmful. As Dr. Burkholder found, that can cause headaches, skin rashes, muscle *cramps*, and loss of memory.

　　另一些人不同意。北卡罗莱那的卫生主管认为没有足够的证据说明幽灵藻威胁到了人类。但是他还是赞扬了伯克霍德的工作并称她是一名"出色的科学工作者"。他知道人们对于幽灵藻有许多疑问。"我们想要得到答案，"他说。

　　一些东西已经知道了，这种微生物不会导致另外一次瘟疫。科研人员说人不会像得伤风流感那样"得"这种病，但是当它的毒素发射出来时附近的人是危险的，此时在水中也是不明智的。科研人员说呼吸毒素的气味也是有害的，如同伯克霍德所发现的那样，这会导致头痛、皮疹、肌肉痉挛和失去记忆。

---

threat　n. 威胁　　　　　　　　　　　　　plague　n. 瘟疫；祸患
cramp　n. 痉挛；抽筋

Some people, though, can't avoid the *fumes*. Shipbuilders and fishermen are around the water all the time. In North Carolina, about 100 of these people seem to have been affected by Pfiesteria blooms. One shipbuilder said, "I had sores ... for over a month, stomach cramping, and shaking."

The state of North Carolina is taking the threat to humans seriously. State officials keep watch on rivers and bays. If there is a fish kill, they post warning signs urging people not to swim, fish, or boat on the water. Sometimes the state just shuts down certain *waterways*. People are not allowed on them until the danger has passed. So even if "the cell from hell" hasn't killed anyone yet, it has caused a lot of waves.

但是一些人无法避开这些毒气。造船工人和渔民总是在水域附近工作。在北卡罗莱那，大约有100名这样的人好像是受到了幽灵藻旺盛发展的影响。一位造船工人说，"我的嘴里……满是溃疡，肚子绞痛，而且发抖。"

北卡罗莱那州认真对待这种对人类的威胁。州的官员紧密关注着河流和海湾，如果出现鱼类死亡的情况他们就会登出警示标语，要求人们不要去游泳、捕鱼或者在此水域划船。有时州政府就把整个水道关闭，在危险解除前，人们是不允许通过的。所以即使"地狱的细胞"没有杀死任何人，它们也导致了许多浪花。

---

fume *n.* 烟气；烟   waterway *n.* 水路；航道

16

The Case of the Missing Pilot

"**I**s there any known *traffic* below five thousand [feet]?" asked Frederick Valentich, a 20-year-old *pilot*.

"No known traffic," answered air traffic control official Steve Robey.

It was October 21, 1978. Valentich was flying a single-engine Cessna plane from Melbourne, Australia, to

On the night Frederick Valentich disappeared, Steve Robey was tracking air traffic on a monitor like this one. The object that Valentich described did not appear on Robey's monitor.

离奇失踪

在弗里德里克·维伦迪克消失的夜晚，斯蒂夫·罗比正在这样的监视器前监视空中交通。维伦迪克描述的物体并没有出现在罗比的显示屏上。

"在5000[英尺]下有没有已经知道的交通运输？"弗里德里克·维伦迪克，一位20岁的飞行员问道。

"没有已知的交通，"飞行交通控制官员斯蒂夫·罗比回答道。

当时是1978年10月21日。维伦迪克正在驾驶一架单引擎凯思那型飞机从澳大利亚的墨尔本飞往国王岛。他在晚上6:30前起飞，飞行计划包括

traffic *n.* 交通   pilot *n.* 飞行员

King Island. He had taken off shortly before 6:30 P.M.. His flight plan called for him to fly over Bass Strait. It was not supposed to be a long flight. It should have taken less than 70 minutes.

But at 7:06 P.M., Valentich saw something outside his *cockpit* window. He radioed the control tower to find out if there were any other planes in the area.

Valentich told Robey he saw what looked like "a large aircraft below five thousand [feet]."

"What type of aircraft is it?" asked Robey.

"I cannot *affirm*," Valentich radioed. He noted that it had four bright lights that looked like landing lights. Then he added, "The aircraft has just passed over me at least a thousand feet above." He said it was traveling too fast for him to tell how big it was.

飞越巴斯海峡。这本不应该是一次长途的飞行，应该在70分钟之内。

但是在晚上7:06的时候，维伦迪克在他驾驶舱玻璃前面看到了什么东西。他给控制台发送无线电信号询问当地是否还有其他的飞机。

维伦迪克告诉罗比说他见到了一个看起来像是在5000[英尺]以下飞行的大型飞行器。

"是什么类型的飞行器？"罗比询问道。

"我也无法确定，"维伦迪克无线电回答道。他注意到它有四个明亮的灯光，看起来像是起落使用的灯光。然后他继续说："那个飞行器就在我的上空1000英尺的地方飞过。"他说它飞得太快了，无法讲述它有多大。

---

cockpit *n.* 驾驶舱   affirm *v.* 断言；肯定

As Valentich and Robey talked, Valentich again asked if there were any planes in the air near him. Again Robey *assured* him that there were "no known aircraft."

But whatever it was, it was still *visible* out Valentich's window. "It's approaching now from due east towards me," Valentich said. "It seems to me that [the pilot is] playing some sort of game. He's flying over me two or three times at speeds I could not identify."

"What is your actual level?" asked Robey.

"My level is four and a half thousand [feet]. Four five zero zero."

Then Valentich radioed another message—one that stunned Steve Robey. "It's not an aircraft," Valentich said.

Robey asked him to describe whatever it was. But the object was still moving too fast for Valentich to get a good look.

　　在维伦迪克和罗比交谈时，维伦迪克开始询问空中在他附近有没有飞机。罗比再次确定地说："没有已知的飞行器。"
　　但是无论它是什么，从维伦迪克的机窗上都可以见到。"现在它从正东方向向我飞来了，"维伦迪克说，"我看好像[那个飞行员]在玩某种游戏，它两三次以我无法确定的速度飞过了我的头顶。"
　　"你的真实高度是多少？"罗比问道。
　　"我的高度是四千五百[英尺]。四、五、零、零。"
　　然后维伦迪克的无线电发出了另一个信息——这使斯蒂夫·罗比很震惊。维伦迪克说："它不是飞机。"
　　罗比请他描述它是什么东西。但是它移动得太快了，维伦迪克无法很好地看清楚。

---

assure　*v.* 使确定　　　　　　　　　　　　visible　*adj.* 看得见的；可见的

"It's a long shape," Valentich radioed. "Cannot identify more than [that because] it has such speed. It's before me right now."

"How large would the—er—object be?" asked Robey.

Valentich did not respond to that question. He was too *focused* on what was happening outside his window. As he watched, the object suddenly appeared to stop moving. "It seems like it's *stationary*," Valentich announced. "What I'm doing right now is *orbiting*, and the thing is just orbiting on top of me. Also, it's got a green light and [is] sort of metallic. It's all shiny on the outside."

The incident was becoming more and more bizarre. After a few seconds, Valentich reported that the object had vanished. Then it came back, this time flying at him from the southwest.

Just at that moment Valentich began to have trouble with his

"是一个长的，"维伦迪克无线电回答道，"其他的无法确定，（因为）它的速度太快，现在又到我的前面去了。"

"那个……物体能有多大？"罗比问道。

维伦迪克没有回答那个问题。他太专注于窗外发生的事情了。他正在看，那个物体突然停止了移动。"看起来它好像突然定住了，"维伦迪克说，"我现在的动作是旋转，那个东西就在我的上空旋转。它上面有一个绿灯而且发出了金属的光泽，整个外观都在闪耀发光。"

整个事件变得越来越奇怪。过了几秒钟后，维伦迪克报告说那个物体消失了，然后又回来了，这次是从西南方向朝着他飞过来的。

就在那时，维伦迪克的飞机出现了问题。"发动机正在空转，"他报

---

focus *v.* 集中　　　　　　　　　　　stationary *adj.* 不动的；静止的
orbit *v.* 沿轨道运行；围绕……运动

plane. "The engine is rough idling," he reported. "I've got it set at twenty three twenty four, and the thing is coughing."

Robey asked Valentich what he planned to do.

"My intentions are—ah—to go to King Island," he answered. "That strange aircraft is hovering on top of me again. It is *hovering*, and it's not an aircraft."

For the next 17 seconds Valentich's *microphone* remained on. But he didn't say anything more. All Robey heard was a metallic scraping sound. After that, there was nothing but silence. That was the last anyone ever heard from Frederick Valentich.

When Valentich failed to show up on King Island, Australian officials started to look for him and his plane. The sky was clear and the winds were light, so weather did not *hamper* the search. It would not have been a *factor* in Valentich's disappearance either. For four

---

告说。"我把它设定为2324，发动机在咳嗽。"

罗比问维伦迪克他打算怎么做。

"我的目的是——啊——到国王岛上去，"他回答道，"那个奇怪的飞行器现在又在我的头上盘旋了，它在盘旋，而且也不是一架飞行器。"

在以后的17秒里面，维伦迪克的麦克风还是打开的状态。但是他什么也没有说。罗比听到的就是金属的摩擦声音，然后就什么也没有了，只有沉寂。那是人们最后听到的弗里德里克·维伦迪克的声音。

维伦迪克没有在国王岛出现，澳大利亚的官方开始搜索他和他的飞机。天空晴朗，而且风很小，这样的天气没有妨碍搜索行动，而且在维伦迪克消失的事件中这也不是个因素。整整四天，搜索人员找遍了巴斯海

---

hover *v.* 盘旋　　　　　　　　　　microphone *n.* 麦克风
hamper *v.* 妨碍；阻止　　　　　　factor *n.* 因素

days searchers *scoured* the Bass Strait. They found nothing. The plane had a radio beacon that was supposed to give out a signal in case of trouble. But no signal was ever sent.

Searchers did find an oil *slick* about 18 miles north of King Island. Could this have been where Valentich's plane had crashed into Bass Strait? Tests showed that the oil was not *aviation* fuel. So the slick couldn't have been from the plane. So what happened to the pilot and the plane? After all these years, that's still an unanswered question. Some people believe that an unidentified flying object—a UFO—was somehow involved. Paul Norman of the Victorian UFO Research Society thinks so. Said Norman, "There is no doubt in my mind that the disappearance of Frederick Valentich and his Cessna was caused by a UFO."

Norman pointed out that other people saw strange things in the

---

峡。他们什么也没有找到。他的飞机上有一个无线电报警器，当遇到麻烦时会报警的，但是当时却没有发出一点信息。

搜索人员在国王岛的北面18英里处的海上发现了一道油迹，这就是维伦迪克飞机坠入巴斯海峡的地点吗？检测表明这个油不是航空燃料油，所以这个油迹不是飞机的。那么飞行员和飞机发生了什么事情呢？多年过去了，这仍然是个未解之谜。一些人认为是不明飞行物——UFO——参与到了其中。维多利亚UFO研究学会的保罗·诺曼是这样认为的。诺曼说："我认为毫无疑问弗里德里克·维伦迪克和他的凯思那飞机的失踪是由UFO导致的。"

诺曼指出，在同一天，还有人在巴斯海峡上空看到了奇怪的景象。大

---

scour *v.* 搜寻某人（某物）　　　　　　　　slick *n.* （海上）浮油
aviation *n.* 航空

sky over Bass Strait that same day. About 2:00 P.M., a woman saw an odd object moving west across the sky. It stopped and hovered for a few minutes. Then it took off again, this time heading east.

Two hours later, another woman and her son saw two cigar-shaped objects move silently through the sky. The objects were silver at first, and then became white. Right after that they turned sharply and shot off.

More sightings came between 7:00 and 8:00 P.M. That was right around the time Valentich disappeared. Some people saw a glowing object that seemed to change from red to pink to white. Others saw something that was shaped like a starfish and gave off a low *pulsating* hum. Yet another eyewitness saw an object that did

---

约下午2:00，一个妇女看到一个奇怪的物体在空中移动。它停下来，盘旋了几分钟，然后又出发了，这次是向东。

两个小时以后，另外一名妇女和她的儿子看到两个雪茄状的物体寂静无声地穿过了天空。刚开始这些物体是银色的，然后变成了白色，然后他们转弯，箭一般地消失了。

晚上7:00到8:00点间更多情况出现了。那正是维伦迪克消失的时间。有人见到一个发光的物体从红色变成了粉色然后白色，还有一些人见到了一个像海星形状的东西，发出了低沉的搏动型嗡嗡声，还有人见到一个物

---

pulsate *v.* 搏动；跳动

"impossible *acrobatics*" for five minutes and then flew off.

One group of witnesses even saw what may have been Valentich's plane with a UFO hovering above it. A man was hunting rabbits with his son and two nieces near Bass Strait. One of the girls looked up and saw a green light in the sky. "What is that light?" she asked.

"An airplane light," answered her uncle. "No," said the niece, "The light above the airplane."

The uncle didn't have an answer to her question.

No one else had any answers either. In 1982, the government of Australia issued its official report. It said the *exact* spot where the plane disappeared was not known. The exact time was not known

---

体做出了"不可能的特技表演"大约5分钟左右，然后飞走了。

一些目击者甚至看到了维伦迪克的飞机上面有UFO在盘旋。一个人带着儿子和两个侄女在巴斯海峡附近打兔子。一个女孩抬头看到了天上有绿色光，"那是什么光？"她问道。

"一架飞机的光，"她的叔叔回答道。"不是，"女孩说，"那个飞机上面的光。"

叔叔没有做出回答。

其他人也没有回答。1982年，澳大利亚政府发布了一个官方的报告。飞机消失的确切地点是未知的，确切的时间也是未知的。实际上，整

---

acrobatics *n.* 杂技   exact *adj.* 精确的

either. In fact, the whole thing was a mystery. In the words of the report, "The reason for the disappearance of the aircraft has not been determined."

The report assumed that whatever had happened, Valentich had died. But no one knows that for sure. Perhaps Valentich faked his own death. Perhaps he became disoriented and flew in the wrong direction, crashing where search parties did not look. Perhaps he was even *abducted* by the object he saw. In the end, all we really know is that Frederick Valentich and his plane *disappeared* into thin air on October 21, 1978. It doesn't seem likely that we will ever know more than that.

个事件都是个谜。按照报告的说法："这次飞机失踪的原因是未知的。"

报告断定，无论发生了什么事情，维伦迪克死了。但是没有人确切地知道，也许是维伦迪克伪造了他的死亡，也许他无法确认方向，飞向错误的方向，坠毁在搜索队没有找到的地方，也许他被他见到的物体绑架了。最终，我们知道的就是弗里德里克·维伦迪克和他的飞机在1978年10月21日消失在稀薄的空气里，看起来我们无法了解比这个更多的信息。

---

abduct *v.* 绑架   disappear *v.* 消失

17

What Happened to Jimmy Hoffa?

Some people *adored* him. Other people *despised* him. With Jimmy Hoffa, there seemed to be no middle ground. In 1957 Hoffa became president of the Teamsters, a union of truckers. He ruled the union with an iron *fist*. Hoffa demanded high wages for his people. That made many members love him. But his enemies claimed he was ruthless.

A happy Jimmy Hoffa smiles at reporters as he leaves a federal prison after serving part of his sentence. Four years later, he disappeared without a trace. Was Hoffa murdered? If so, why was his body never found?

神秘失踪

快乐的吉米·霍法向记者们报以微笑。此时，刑期未满的他离开了联邦监狱。四年之后，他消失了，没有留下任何踪迹。他被谋杀了吗？如果是这样，为什么人们从未发现过他的尸首呢？

有些人很喜爱他，有些人很蔑视他。对于吉米·霍法，似乎并没有站在中间立场上的人。1957年，霍法成为一个卡车驾驶员的组织——也就是卡车司机工会的主席。他用铁腕方式管理着这个工会。霍法为他旗下的人们申请到了更高的工资待遇，由此得到了众多会员的爱戴。但是他的敌

adore *v.* 爱慕；喜爱　　　　　　　　　　despise *v.* 蔑视；轻视
fist *n.* 拳头

Anyone who crossed him had to watch out. They might be beaten up or *harassed* in other ways.

Hoffa's enemies were right. Hoffa was more than a union leader. He was also a *crook*. He had close ties to "the mob," or organized crime. More than once, the federal government tried to prove that Hoffa was *corrupt* and was taking advantage of his union. At last, in 1964, Hoffa lost two trials. He was found guilty of *tampering* with a jury. He was also found guilty of taking union money for his own use. Hoffa made several appeals. But he lost them all. In 1967 he began to serve a 13-year sentence in prison.

Hoffa did not just roll over and play dead, though. He found a way to run the Teamsters from behind bars. He used his son, James, as a go-between. "He was like a caged lion in prison," said James later. "All he talked about was his union."

人攻击他是一个残酷无情的人。任何与他有交往的人都要小心提防，因为他可能会利用其他手段打击或者骚扰他们。

霍法的敌人们是正确的。霍法不仅仅是一名工会领导人，更是一个大骗子。他与"乱党"有着紧密的联系，或许他也曾经参与过某些犯罪组织的活动。联邦政府曾经不止一次地试图证明霍法有腐败行为，而且从他的工会中牟取利益。最后，霍法输掉了两场官司。他被发现犯有干涉陪审员工作，以及挪工会钱财为己用的罪行。霍法进行了数次上诉，但全部以失败告终。1967年，他开始了在狱中13年的服刑。

但是霍法并没有苟且度日。他找到一种在幕后操控卡车司机工会的方法。他利用儿子詹姆士充当了中间人。詹姆士后来说道："他就像被困在笼子里的狮子，他说的全都是有关工会的话题。"

---

harass *v.* 使烦恼；使困扰

corrupt *adj.* 腐败的

crook *n.* 骗子

tamper *v.* 干涉；干预

In 1971 Hoffa was *paroled*. After serving just four years of his sentence, he was freed. But there was a string attached to his freedom. He could not hold any union office for nine years. (That was the time left on his sentence.) This deal had been set up by Frank Fitzsimmons, the union's vice president.

It is not clear why Fitzsimmons acted as he did. Maybe he was just trying to help Hoffa. Or maybe he was trying to limit Hoffa's power. In any case, Hoffa did not know about the deal until after he was free. He hated it. He felt Fitzsimmons had *double-crossed* him.

Hoffa spent the next four years trying to get the *ban* lifted. He fought Fitzsimmons for control of the Teamsters. Some members of the mob supported Hoffa. Others threw their support to Fitzsimmons.

On July 30, 1975, Hoffa planned to meet some *gangsters* for

1971年，霍法被假释出狱。仅仅服刑4年之后，他就自由了。但是他的这种自由有一个附加的限制，那就是9年（就是他余下的那些刑期）之内他不能担当任何工会职务。这个条件是由工会副主席弗兰克·菲茨孟斯提出的。

菲茨孟斯这样做的原因不很清楚。也许他仅仅是试图帮助霍法，也许他是想限制霍法的权力。不管怎样，霍法直到获得自由之后才知道这个附加条件。他怀恨在心，觉得菲茨孟斯背叛了他。

霍法花了4年时间试图撤销这个禁令。他与菲茨孟斯为工会的控制权展开了斗争。有些"乱党"成员支持他，另外一些人支持菲茨孟斯。

1975年7月30日，霍法计划设午宴款待一些犯罪分子。他希望在与菲

---

parole v. 假释；宣誓后释放　　　　　double-cross v. 欺骗
ban n. 禁令　　　　　　　　　　　　gangster n. 歹徒；流氓

lunch. He hoped to win their support in his fight with Fitzsimmons. The men were supposed to meet at a restaurant near Detroit. Hoffa got there first. He waited patiently, but the gangsters never showed up. After a few hours, Hoffa called home. Had they left a message for him? They had not. One *witness* saw Hoffa leave the restaurant. He was in the back seat of a car with some other men. It was the last time anyone ever saw the 62-year-old union leader.

Hoffa's son, James, remembered what happened the next morning. "My mother called about 6:30 A.M.. She told me that [my father] hadn't come home. Right away I *expected* the worst." In other words, James believed his father had been killed.

The police agreed. But they had no *proof*. Hoffa's body was never found. At first, the police got lots of *tips*. They looked for his body

---

茨孟斯的斗争中得到他们的支持。他准备在底特律附近的一家饭店招待这些人。霍法先期到达那里。他耐心地等待着，但这些犯罪分子没有露面。几小时之后，霍法回到家中。他们给他留下什么讯息了吗？没有。一位目击者看到霍法离开了那家饭店，与另外几名男子坐在一辆小汽车的后座上。这是最后一次有人看到这位62岁的工会领导人。

霍法的儿子，詹姆士，还记得第二天早晨发生的事情。"大概是早上六点半，我妈妈给我打电话，说我爸爸没回家。我马上就想到了最坏的情况。"换句话说，詹姆士相信他的父亲被杀害了。

警方同意这种看法，但是他们没有证据。从来没有人见过霍法的尸体。最初，警方得到很多秘密消息，到处寻找霍法的尸首。他们挖开了玉

---

witness *n.* 目击者；证人

proof *n.* 证据；证明

expect *v.* 预料；期望

tip *n.* 秘诀；技巧

everywhere. They dug up cornfields. They drilled through *concrete* floors. They checked rivers and lakes. But their searches always came up empty.

Meanwhile, *weird* rumors about Hoffa kept floating about. Some people believed that the mob had cut up his body and dropped the pieces in a *swamp*. Others claimed he was buried under the goalposts at Giants Stadium in New Jersey. Still others said his body was put in a car crusher. The best bet might be that his killers dropped him into a vat of boiling *zinc*. That was how the Detroit mob often got rid of a murder victim.

Only the killers know the true story. But none of them are talking. And unless one of them does talk, the rest of us will never know what really happened to Jimmy Hoffa.

米地，钻开了水泥地面，也在河流湖泊中搜查了一番。但是他们这些调查的结果总是两手空空。

与此同时，一些关于霍法离奇失踪的流言开始传播。有人相信是那些乱党分子将他的尸身肢解，并把那些碎片扔到一个沼泽中。有人声称他被埋在新泽西巨人体育场的门柱下面。有人说他的尸体被扔到了车辆破碎机里。可能性最大的是，杀害他的那个人把他扔进一个装有金属锌的大桶里。这是底特律的匪帮除掉谋杀对象最常用的方法。

只有那些凶手知道真相，但是他们谁都没有谈起过。除非他们当中有人说出这个事实，否则我们永远不会知道吉米·霍法到底遇到了什么事情。

---

concrete *n.* 混凝土；水泥
swamp *n.* 沼泽；湿地

weird *adj.* 怪异的；不可思议的
zinc *n.* 锌

18

The Truth About the Tasaday

Could a Stone Age tribe *survive* into the 20th century? It didn't seem possible. By 1970 almost every place on Earth had been fully *explored*. How could any group be living *unnoticed* by the rest of the world? But in 1971 an *amazing* thing happened. A Stone Age tribe was

Philippine official Manuel Elizalde learns about the peaceful ways of a primitive tribe of people called the Tasaday, with the help of a local interpreter. These happy people seemed too good to be true—for a very good reason.

塔萨代人真相

在当地翻译的协助下，菲律宾官员曼纽尔·艾力扎得掌握了与一个原始部落和平相处的方法，这个部落是由被称作塔萨代人的原始人组成的。这些快乐的人看上去状态是那么好，以至于——似乎有充足的理由认为——他们是不真实的。

一个处于石器时代的部落能够生存在20世纪吗？这一点看上去是不可能的。到了1970年，地球上几乎每一个角落都被完全探测过了。又怎么可能有任何一群人，在从未被世人注意过的情况下生存着呢？但是，1971年发生了一件令人惊异的事情，一个仍旧处于石器时代的部落被发

survive *v.* 幸存；生存
unnoticed *adj.* 不引人注意的

explore *v.* 探测；探索
amazing *adj.* 令人惊异的

found. The name of the tribe was the Tasaday. Experts everywhere were *thrilled* by this discovery.

How did the Tasaday stay unknown for so long? First, the tribe was tiny. It *contained* just 26 people. Second, they lived in deep caves. Third, their home was in a rain forest deep in the Philippines. And fourth, they made all the things they needed, so they had no reason to *seek* outside trading partners.

The Tasaday were discovered by a local *trapper*. He said he came upon them one day while hunting. The trapper told Manuel Elizalde, a Philippine official. Soon the word got out. Several experts came to see the tribe. They were eager to study the Tasaday. After all, these people knew nothing about the modern world. Visiting them was like traveling back in time. It allowed researchers to see how humans

现了。这个部落叫作塔萨代。世界各地的专家都被这一发现惊呆了。

塔萨代人怎么可能存在了那么长时间却无人知晓呢？首先，这个部落非常小，仅由26人组成。其次，他们住在深深的洞穴里。第三，他们的家在菲律宾热带雨林深处。第四，他们完全是自力更生的，因此没有向外界寻找贸易伙伴的理由。

塔萨代人是被当地一位猎手发现的。他说是有一天在打猎时遇到他们的。这位猎手把这一情况告诉了曼纽尔·艾力扎得，一位菲律宾政府官员。消息很快就传开了。有几位专家前来考察这个部落。他们热切地希望研究一下塔萨代人。毕竟，这些人对现代社会一无所知。探访他们就仿佛是在时间中

thrill v. 感到兴奋或激动
seek v. 寻找；探索

contain v. 包含；容纳
trapper n. 捕捉动物的人

had lived long, long ago.

National Geographic fell in love with the Tasaday. The magazine did several stories on the tribe as it "stepped out of the Stone Age." Then came books, movies, and TV specials. Everyone, it seemed, adored these *innocent* people.

What were the Tasaday like? They wore very little clothing. What they did wear they wove from tree leaves. They did not know how to grow their own food. They had never seen rice, corn, or sugar. One expert said they could be "the only people in the world today who do not know or use tobacco." The Tasaday kept no *domestic* animals, either. They survived by eating wild palms, yams, crabs, and tadpoles. And, of course, the Tasaday had no *metal*. That is why they were called "Stone Age" people. Their only tools came from

---

倒行。这个调查可以让研究者们观察到人类很久很久以前是如何生活的。

　　《国家地理》杂志十分倾心于塔萨代人。这个杂志作了好几期关于这个部落的"走出石器时代"的报道，然后又陆续出版了书籍、电影和电视特别节目。似乎每一个人都特别喜欢这些纯朴的人们。

　　塔萨代人有什么特征呢？他们只穿很少的衣服，是用树叶为原料编织而成的衣物。他们不知道如何种植粮食，从未见过大米、玉米或者糖料。一位专家说，他们可能是"当今世界上仅有的不了解或使用烟草的人"。塔萨代人也没有驯养的动物。他们以吃野棕榈、山药、螃蟹和蝌蚪为生。当然，他们没有金属工具。这就是他们被称作"石器时代"的人的原因。

---

fall in love with　爱上；喜欢
domestic　*adj.*　驯养的

innocent　*adj.*　无辜的；清白的
metal　*n.*　金属

stone.

The Tasaday were very peaceful. Their sweet nature won the hearts of all those who saw them. The tribe had no words for "weapon" or "war" or "enemy." As one writer put it, "If our ancestors were like the Tasaday, we came from far better *stock* than I believed." It seemed that these Stone Age people might have a lot to teach the rest of us.

The goal, then, was to protect the Tasaday. That was Elizalde's job. He was *in charge of* protecting all the tribes in the Philippines. He did not want the Tasaday's way of life *ruined*. He feared that would happen if too many people came to visit. So he sent soldiers to guard the caves. Just a few people were allowed in. And first they had to be *approved* by Elizalde. Because of this rule, few scientists

---

他们仅有的工具都是用石头制作的。

塔萨代人非常平和。他们友善的天性赢得了所有见过他们的人的心。这个部落的语言里没有"武器"、"战争"和"敌人"。正如一位作家笔下的,"如果我们的祖先像塔萨代人一样,我们就会拥有比我现在所认为的更好的血统。"似乎这些石器时代的人教会我们很多东西。

这样一来,人们的目标就是保护塔萨代人。这就是艾力扎得的工作。他负责保护菲律宾境内所有的原始部落。他不想让塔萨代人的这种生活方式彻底消失。他担心如果有太多人前去参观,那么上述情况就不可避免,所以就派士兵前去保卫那些洞穴,只有少数人被允许进入其中,并且事先必须得到艾力扎得本人批准。由于这条规定的存在,只有少数科学家前去

---

stock *n.* 血统
ruin *v.* 毁灭;毁坏

in charge of 负责;主管
approve *v.* 批准

got to see the tribe. And that's the way things stayed until 1986.

Meanwhile, the Tasaday seemed to look on Elizalde as a god. "Our ancestors told us never to leave this place of ours," said one. "They told us the god of our people would come. Their words have been proven true by the coming of [Elizalde]." The Tasaday even gave him a new name. It was Mono Dakel de Weta Tasaday. That meant "Great Man, God of the Tasaday."

But as time passed, rumors began to *spread*. Some people started to have doubts about the tribe. One person *claimed* he saw cooked rice being *sneaked* into the caves. Others said they saw the Tasaday wearing clothes. Still others *maintained* they had seen tribe members smoking cigarettes. Few people listened to these reports, however. Belief in the "Stone Age" tribe ran too deep.

探看了这个部落。这种情况一直持续到1986年。

　　此时，塔萨代人似乎把艾力扎得看作一个神。部落里的一个人说："我们的祖先告诫我们不要离开这片土地。他们告诉我们会有至高无上的神来到这里。他[艾力扎得]的到来证明他们祖先的话是正确的。"塔萨代人给他起了一个新名字，叫作塔萨代的摩诺德柯维塔，意思是"伟人，塔萨代的上帝"。

　　但是，随着时间的流逝，许多传闻开始流传出来。有些人开始怀疑这个部落的存在。有人宣称看见过有人把做熟的米饭偷偷拿进洞穴中，有人说他们看见过塔萨代人穿着衣服，还有人坚持说曾经看见过部落成员抽着香烟。然而很少有人听说过此类报道。对这个"石器时代"部落的信任感已经深入人心了。

---

spread v. 流传；传播

sneak v. 偷偷地做

claim v. 宣称；声称

maintain v. 坚持；主张

Then, in 1986, a huge change took place in the Philippines. The old government was swept away. A new, freer one was set up. Even before the old *regime* ended, Elizalde slipped out of sight. He simply *vanished*. It was said that he fled the country. He took $35 million with him. It was money that he was supposed to have used to aid tribes like the Tasaday.

When the old government *crumbled*, so did the *shield* around the Tasaday. Now outsiders could see for themselves who these people really were. A Swiss writer named Oswald Iten went looking for the Tasaday. He found their caves empty. He did, however, find the very same "Stone Age" people a short distance away. They were living in comfortable huts. They were wearing T-shirts and jeans. And they were using metal knives.

然而，1986年，菲律宾发生了一次巨大的变化。前政府被推翻，一个新的自由的政府建立起来。甚至是在旧政权倒台之前，艾力扎就从人们的视线中淡出了。他完全销声匿迹了。据说他潜逃到其他国家去了，随身带走了3500万美金，这些钱原本是应该用于资助像塔萨代这样的原始部落的。

原政府垮台了，塔萨代的保护伞也没有了。现在外界人士可以亲自去看看这里的人们究竟是什么情况。一位瑞士作家奥斯瓦德·艾登去寻找塔萨代这个部落。他发现他们的洞穴里空空如也。但是他说在一个很近的距离之内看到同样的"石器时代"的人类。他们住在舒适的小屋里，穿着圆领汗衫和牛仔裤，使用的是金属刀具。

---

regime *n.* 政权；政体   vanish *v.* 消失；突然不见

crumble *v.* 垮台；崩溃   shield *n.* 防护；起保护作用的人或物

Iten realized that the whole tribe was *nothing but* a hoax. The people claiming to be Tasaday really came from two other tribes. These tribes had been part of the modern world for many, many years.

Soon others picked up the story. ABC did a TV special. It was called "The Tribe That Never Was." It showed the Tasaday laughing as they looked at photos of themselves from *National Geographic*. Tasaday supporters now faced *tough* questions. Why were the caves so clean? Where were the crab shells and *scraps* of food? Even Stone Age tribes had garbage, didn't they?

Besides, how could such a small tribe sustain itself? Wouldn't the Tasaday have needed *spouses* from the outside? Scientists said a tribe living on its own would need at least 400 members, not 26. The

---

艾登意识到整个部落不过是一个骗局。声称是塔萨代人的那些人其实来自另外两个部落，而这些部落成为现代世界的一部分已经很多很多年了。

很快其他人捕捉到了这件事情。美国广播公司做了一期电视特别节目，名为"从未出现过的部落"。这个节目显示塔萨代人看到他们自己在《国家地理》杂志上的照片时正在发笑。塔萨代的支持者们现在面临着严峻的问题。那些洞穴为什么那么干净？那些蟹壳和残羹剩饭哪去了？就连石器时代的部落都会有垃圾，那他们的呢？

除此之外，这么小的一个部落是如何维系自身存在的？难到塔萨代人不需要与外界通婚吗？科学家说一个部落要想自力更生地存在下来至少需

---

nothing but 只有；只不过
scrap *n.* 残余物

tough *adj.* 困难的；严峻的
spouse *n.* 配偶

Tasaday said they sometimes married people from two other Stone Age tribes. But these other tribes were never found.

Finally, the Tasaday caves were just a three-hour walk from an *established* village. How come no one from the tribe ever walked there? Had their search for food never brought them near the village? It *made no sense*—unless the tribe was a *fake*. One expert called the Tasaday "rain forest clock punchers." They went to work as "cave people" in the morning. At night, after the visitors left, they went back to their village homes.

Who was behind this fraud? The finger points to Elizalde. He made lots of money from his scheme to "protect" the Tasaday. The "Tasaday" agreed to go along with him because they were poor. They were told they could make some money by putting on a show.

要400个人，而不是26个人。塔萨代人说他们有时会嫁娶另外两个石器时代部落的人，但是人们从来没有找到过那些部落。

　　最后一个问题是，塔萨代人的洞穴与一个早已建成的村庄间的距离只需步行3个小时。为什么这个部落的人从来没有走到过那个村庄去呢？难道他们在寻找食物的时候就从未接近过那个村庄吗？完全没有道理——除非这个部落本身是伪造的。一位专家说塔萨代人是"热带雨林中的定时穿梭者"。夜间，在参观者离开之后，他们回到他们在村庄里的家。

　　这个骗局的幕后操纵者是谁？矛头指向艾力扎得。他从他的"保护"塔萨代计划中捞取了很多钱财。"塔萨代人"同意配合他的行动，因为他们非常贫穷。艾力扎得告诉他们经过这样的伪装，他们能够得到一些金

---

established *adj.* 早已确立的；老牌的　　　　make no sense 毫无意义
fake *n.* 骗子；假货

"Elizalde said if we went *naked* we'd get [money] because we'd look poor," one man explained.

The Tasaday *put on* a great act. They fooled everyone for a while. Even the so-called experts fell for the *scam*. But we now know that the Tasaday are not a real Stone Age tribe. If such a tribe does still *exist*, no one has found it yet.

钱。一位男子解释说："艾力扎得说如果我们赤身裸体，就能拿到钱，因为我们看上去很穷。"

塔萨代人上演了一场好戏。他们在一定时间内欺骗了每一个人。甚至所谓的专家都中了这个诡计。但是现在，我们知道塔萨代不是一个真实存在的石器时代的部落。如果这样一个部落确实存在，那么至今还没有人发现它。

---

naked *adj.* 裸体的
scam *n.* 骗局；诡计

put on 上演
exist *v.* 存在

19

Lost for 16 Years

Patti White Bull *checked* into the hospital on June 12, 1983. "I'll see you tomorrow" she told her nine-year-old daughter, Cindy. By then, Patti thought, she would have *given birth to* her fourth child. She would be able to show Cindy a brand new brother or sister.

How would it feel to wake up after 16 years in a coma? Less than two months after her recovery, Patti White Bull tests her ability to walk with the help of a volunteer and a physical therapist.

遗失的16年

昏迷16年之后苏醒时会是什么感觉？痊愈之后不到两个月，在一名志愿者和一名物理治疗专家的协助下，帕蒂·怀特·布尔试验着她走路的能力。

1983年6月12日，帕蒂·怀特·布尔入院检查。她告诉9岁的女儿辛迪："我明天就会来看你。"当时，帕蒂以为她就要生第四个孩子了。她会带给辛迪一个弟弟或妹妹。

---

check *v.* 检查　　　　　　　　　　　　give birth to　生孩子

Patti and her husband, Mark, already had three children. Besides Cindy, there were three-year-old Jesse and one-year-old Floris. So while Patti went to the hospital in Albuquerque, New Mexico, Mark *cared for* the three children. That night he took them to work with him.

By the next morning, Mark was eager to join Patti. But first he had to make a quick stop at their house in Edgewood. There, Mark found a note pinned to the door. That was when he learned something had gone wrong.

Patti had given birth to a healthy baby boy. But a blood clot had formed. It *lodged* in her lung. That caused her to stop breathing. Her heart stopped *pumping* oxygen to her brain. Doctors *scrambled* to

---

帕蒂和她的丈夫马克已经有三个孩子了。除了辛迪，另外两个是三岁的耶西和一岁的弗洛雷斯。所以，当辛迪进入新墨西哥州阿尔伯克一家医院时，马克正在照看其他三个孩子。那天晚上他去工作的时候带上了他们。

第二天早晨，马克急切地想见到帕蒂。但是当他回到埃奇伍德的住宅时，他首先不得不立刻停住了脚步。在那里，马克发现门上别着一个纸条。当时他就意识到一定是出了什么事情。

帕蒂生出一个健康的男孩。但是在她的肺部暂时形成了一个血块，这使得她停止呼吸了。她的心脏停止向脑部供氧。医生对她实行紧急抢救，

---

care for 关心；照顾
pump *v.* 压入气体

lodge *v.* 寄存
scramble *v.* 争夺；争先恐后

save her. But it took six minutes to get her breathing again. By then she was in a *coma*. She could not *respond* to the people around her. She was *unconscious*.

Mark hoped Patti would come out of the coma quickly. But after a few days, her condition had not changed. Sadly, Mark brought Cindy to the hospital to see Patti. Cindy was shocked. She thought of her 27-year-old mother as a beautiful and active woman. Patti White Bull had worked as a model. She had made jewelry and taught yoga. A member of the Pueblo tribe, she had also worked to help other Native Americans. In fact, she had been so *upbeat* that her nickname was Happi.

But now tubes were sticking out of Patti's body. Her eyes were

---

但是花了6分钟才让她恢复了呼吸。此时，她已经处于昏迷状态，不能对周围的人做出反应，已经不省人事了。

马克期望着帕蒂快些从昏迷状态中苏醒过来。但是过了几天，她的状况仍然没有变化。马克非常难过，带着辛迪去医院看望帕蒂。辛迪被眼前的场景惊呆了。她原想她27岁的妈妈是一位漂亮并且充满活力的妇人。帕蒂·怀特·布尔从事过模特工作，做过珠宝生意，教授过瑜伽术。作为普艾布罗一个社团的成员之一，她还从事过救助美国本土人的工作。实际上，她是如此乐观，以致她的昵称就是"小快乐"。

但是现在，帕蒂的身上插着很多管子。她的眼睛是睁着的，但是目光

---

coma *n.* 昏迷
unconscious *adj.* 不省人事的

respond *v.* 回答；做出反应
upbeat *adj.* 乐观的

open, but *vacant*. She did not appear to see anything. She didn't even blink. She could not swallow, so she was being fed through a tube. Her hands were tightly *clenched*. No part of her body moved.

Cindy White Bull was *crushed*. So was Mark. He asked his mother to care for the new baby, named Mark, Jr. Mark and the other children spent many nights sleeping in the bathroom of Patti's hospital room. They all wanted to be there if she woke up.

But the days passed and Patti did not *stir*. She was moved to the Las Palomas Nursing Home. There she remained locked in what doctors called a semi-vegetative state. For two years Mark visited her almost every day. "Sometimes I would try to talk her into waking up," he said. "I'd say, 'You're by a stream now. We're sitting together.

呆滞，好像什么都看不见，她甚至眼睛都不眨一下，也不能吞咽食物，所以只能通过一根管子进食。她的双手紧紧地握着，身上没有哪个部分可以活动。

　　帕蒂·怀特·布尔被击倒了，马克也是如此。他拜托妈妈照看那个新生的孩子，他的名字叫作小马克。在帕蒂病房的盥洗室里，马克和另外几个孩子睡了很多个夜晚。他们都希望一旦她清醒过来，他们都在她的身边。

　　但是，日子一天天过去了，她却一动不动。她被转移到拉斯帕洛玛斯疗养院。在那里，她仍然处在医生称为半植物人的状态中。两年里，马克几乎每天都去探望她。他说："有时候，我和她说话，希望她能醒过来。我说：'你现在在一条小溪边，我们坐在一起。你虽然很累，但现在该醒

---

vacant *adj.* 空的；茫然的　　　　　clenched *adj.* 紧咬的；紧握的
crush *v.* 压垮　　　　　　　　　　　stir *v.* 走动；动弹

You're really tired, but you need to wake up now. The kids need you. I need you...' "

It didn't work. By 1985 Patti still showed no sign of improvement. Finally, Mark decided he had to move on with his life. He asked the courts to *grant* him a divorce. Then he moved to South Dakota. There his mother could help him raise his children.

It was hard for everyone to leave Patti behind. But the doctors said that she wouldn't know the difference. She could not hear them. She could not see them. Doctors expected her to spend the rest of her life in a *catatonic* state.

As the years passed, Mark White Bull struggled to forget Patti. He married and divorced two more times. Meanwhile Cindy and her

---

醒了。孩子需要你。我需要你……' "

但这一切毫无作用。直到1985年，帕蒂仍然没有显示出好转的迹象。最后，马克决定与妻子分开。他要求法院准许他离婚。然后，他搬到了南达科他州。在那里，他的妈妈能够帮助他抚养孩子。

让所有人都对帕蒂弃之不理是很困难的。但是医生说她根本不会体察到这些差别。她听不到他们说话，也看不到他们。医生以为，她只能在这种对刺激毫无反应的状态度过她的余生了。

很多年过去了，马克·怀特·布尔想尽力忘掉帕蒂。他又结过两次婚，然后又都离婚了。与此同时，辛迪和她的弟弟妹妹们都长大了。

---

grant *v.* 允许；授予 catatonic *adj.* 紧张性精神分裂症的

siblings grew up. In 1989 Cindy joined the Marines. By 1999 she was married and had children of her own. Jesse was in college. Floris and Mark, Jr., were teenagers. None of them thought they would ever see their mother awake again.

But four days before Christmas, an amazing thing happened. A nurse's *aide* was fixing the sheets on Patti's bed when *all at once* Patti spoke. "Don't do that!" she exclaimed.

No one at the nursing home could believe it. After 16 years Patti White Bull had woken up.

Within hours Patti was on the phone to her mother. Her voice was *shaky* but clear. "Merry Christmas, Mom," she said.

It took a while to reach the rest of the family. When Mark White

---

1989年，辛迪加入了海军陆战队。1999年，她结了婚，有了自己的孩子。耶西正在上大学。弗洛雷斯和小马克也都十几岁了。他们没有人认为会见到妈妈再次苏醒过来。

但是就在圣诞节前四天，一件神奇的事情发生了。一位护士的助手正在整理帕蒂床上的被单。突然，帕蒂开口讲话了。她大声说道："别那么干！"

疗养院中没有人能够相信这个事实。16年后，帕蒂·怀特·布尔苏醒过来了。

没有几个小时，帕蒂就给妈妈打了电话。她声音微弱，但是很清晰。她说："妈妈，圣诞快乐！"

消息不久就传到了其他家庭成员那里。马克·怀特·布尔听到这个消

---

sibling *n.* 兄弟姊妹　　　　　　　　　　　aide *n.* 助手

all at once 突然　　　　　　　　　　　　　shaky *adj.* 颤抖的

Bull heard the news, he quickly made plans to drive to New Mexico. Jesse, Floris, and Mark, Jr., went with him. Cindy was away on vacation. But when she heard what had happened, she, too, left for New Mexico.

By Christmas morning Patti was able to dress herself. With a little help she could take a few steps. Later that week, when Cindy arrived, Patti held out her arms for a *hug*.

"Her face was lit up," said Cindy.

When Mark, Jr., arrived Patti *murmured*, "Junior?" It was the first time he had ever heard her voice.

Patti's muscles and *vocal chords* were very weak. *In addition*, she showed some signs of brain damage. She needed to learn many

---

息后，立即决定驱车前往新墨西哥。耶西、弗洛雷斯和小马克随他一起上路。辛迪正在外面度假。但是，当她听说发生的事情之后，也动身前往新墨西哥。

到了圣诞节那天早上，帕蒂可以自己穿衣服了。只需少许帮助，她就可以走上几步。当周晚些时候，辛迪赶到时，帕蒂可以举起胳膊，并把两臂抱在一起。

辛迪说："她的脸上重新有了光彩。"

当小马克到来的时候，帕蒂嘴里咕哝着："是小马克吗？"这是他第一次听到妈妈的声音。

帕蒂的肌肉和声带力量仍然非常虚弱。另外，她的大脑似乎受到了某

---

hug *n.* 拥抱
vocal chords 声带

murmur *v.* 低声说
in addition 另外，此外

things all over again. She couldn't brush her hair or wash her hands by herself. Still, it was *astounding* to see what she could do. Within a couple of weeks, she took her first bite of pizza. She tried on some lipstick. Best of all, she gave all her children big hugs.

Dr. Eliot Marcus was in charge of Patti's case. "I cannot come up with a medical explanation," he said. "I have never seen anything like this." Other doctors said the same thing. "It really is quite amazing," said one. Another simply called it "*absolutely extraordinary*."

To this day no one knows what caused Patti White Bull to wake up. But some doctors have a theory. In December 1999 the flu was going around Patti's nursing home. To protect the patients, doctors gave out a flu medicine. It was called amantadine. Patti White Bull

---

种伤害。她需要重新学习很多东西。她还不能自己梳头和洗手。但是，她的所作所为仍然让人大吃一惊。仅仅几周之内，她咬了第一口比萨饼，并试着涂口红。最令人高兴的是，她给了每个孩子大大的拥抱。

埃利奥特·马库斯医生主管帕蒂的病情。他说："我给不出一个医学上的解释。我从来没碰到过类似的情况。"其他医生也这么说。一位医生说："这真是太令人惊奇了"，另一位医生干脆称其为"绝对奇迹"。

直到今天，没有人知道是什么导致了帕蒂·怀特·布尔的苏醒。但是有些医生抱有一种推测。1999年12月，帕蒂的疗养院附近爆发了流感。为了保护病人，医生分发了感冒药，药名叫作金刚烷胺。帕蒂·怀特·布

---

astounding *adj.* 令人震惊的

extraordinary *adj.* 离奇的，非凡的

absolutely *adv.* 绝对地；完全地

was given some of it. Perhaps this medicine *somehow triggered* her recovery.

Once Patti woke up, doctors kept giving her amantadine. They feared that without it, she would go downhill. Even with it, they were not sure what her future held. They warned the family that she could *slip* back into a coma at any time. But the family was happy just to take one day at a time. As Patti's son Jesse said, "Every moment with her is a special moment for me and my brother and sisters. It's something we never had. When you find it, you want to hold it *as long as* you can."

尔也拿到了一些。也许是这种药最终使她痊愈。

帕蒂苏醒之后，医生就坚持让她服用金刚烷胺。他们担心离开它，她的病情会加重。即使坚持用这种药，他们也不敢肯定她今后会如何。他们警告她的家人，帕蒂随时有可能再度陷入昏迷状态。但是即使只有一天时间能和她在一起，家人们也已经非常高兴了。正如帕蒂的儿子耶西所说："对我和我的兄弟姐妹来说，和她在一起的每时每刻都是很特别的。我们从来没遇到过这种事情。一旦你遇到，你就会尽力坚持下去。"

---

somehow *adv.* 莫名其妙地
slip *v.* 减退；倒退

trigger *v.* 触发；引起
as long as 只要